THE INVISIBLE
WEIGHT
WE CARRY

THE INVISIBLE
WEIGHT
WE CARRY

Breaking Free from Generational Burdens
and Emotional Baggage

LARYSSA M. CRESWELL, ED.D

MEDIA.COM

The Invisible Weight We Carry

Copyright © 2025 by Laryssa M. Creswell

Published by
Illumify Media Global
www.IllumifyMedia.com
"Let's bring your book to life!"

Paperback ISBN: 978-1-964251-37-0

Cover design by Debbie Lewis

Printed in the United States of America

DEDICATION

To my mother and my late father, thank you for your unwavering support and for laying the foundation that taught me to believe in the possibility of even my wildest dreams. Your love and strength gave me the courage to leap, knowing you would always be there to catch me should I need you.

Contents

Foreword ix

Introduction 1

SECTION 1: So What's the Problem? 5

Chapter 1: Facing Reality 7

Chapter 2: It Came from Somewhere......................... 23

Section 2: Get Unstuck by Balancing Expectations,

Needs, Wants & Intentions 41

Chapter 3: You Want Me to Do What?........................ 43

Chapter 4: All About You 61

Section 3: Get Unstuck by Reinventing Your Story 83

Chapter 5: The Stories We Tell...................................... 85

Chapter 6: Breaking Down the Story 97

Chapter 7: Rewriting the Story 107

Section 4: Get Unstuck by Creating

    Healing Connections..**121**

Chapter 8: Connect to the Self 123

Chapter 9: Where's My Crew? 135

Chapter 10: Connect with Your Destiny 147

Resources..**163**

Bibliography **165**

About the Author..**167**

Foreword

In a world that often demands we carry our burdens silently, *The Invisible Weight We Carry: Breaking Free from Generational Burdens and Emotional Baggage* arrives as a much-needed guide to self-liberation. The weight of our past—whether inherited from previous generations, shaped by society, or forged through our personal experiences—can be overwhelming, leaving us feeling stuck and powerless. Yet, as Laryssa eloquently reminds us, within each of us lies the power to reclaim our narrative and reshape our future.

I have had the distinct honor of watching Laryssa grow on her professional journey. Time and time again, she has stepped outside of her comfort zone, demonstrating a remarkable commitment to her own growth and healing. Laryssa is a prime example of practicing what she preaches, and this book is a testament to her dedication to helping others find their own path to freedom.

You are invited on a transformative journey of self-discovery and healing, guided by Laryssa's compassionate voice and wealth of experience as a therapist. Her unique blend of therapeutic insight and relatable storytelling offers a beacon of hope to those who have struggled under the invisible weight of trauma, expectations, and societal pressures. The stories and examples resonate with a raw honesty that feels both comforting and challenging, inviting you to confront the parts of yourself you may have kept hidden, to name the burdens you've been carrying, and to finally set them down.

As you turn the pages of this book, you'll find yourself not just reading, but actively participating in a journey toward freedom. The exercises and reflections are thoughtfully designed to help you engage with the material in a way that feels authentic and deeply personal. Laryssa's guidance is gentle yet firm, encouraging you to dig deep, to question long-held beliefs, and to embrace the possibility of a life unburdened by the past.

This book is a gift to anyone who has ever felt weighed down by life's challenges. It offers a roadmap to a place of self-compassion, resilience, and ultimately, freedom. As you embark on this journey, remember that you have always had the power to rewrite your story—this book will simply help you find it.

I'll leave you with a poem as you set out on your continued healing journey.

Unburdened

 Lay down the weight you've carried long,

 In shadows deep where fears belong.

 Release the chains of yesteryears,

 And let them melt like morning tears.

 The past is but a whispered sigh,

 A story told beneath the sky.

 But now, the sun is breaking through,

 A path of light awaits for you.

 With every step, you shed the old,

 And in your heart, new dreams unfold.

 You are the writer of your tale,

 And in this life, you will prevail.

 So walk with courage, stand with grace,

 And let the wind kiss your face.

 For you are free, unburdened, whole,

 The keeper of your sacred soul.

Carly Hill

xoxo

Introduction

I just love *The Wiz*. All of it: the music, the storytelling, the glitz.

And, oh my goodness, my childhood crush Michael Jackson singing "You Can't Win," still makes me smile and hum the song in my head.

But here's my absolute favorite moment in the movie: when Glinda, the good witch, says, "You've always had the power, my dear, you just had to learn it for yourself." *Yesssss, Glinda!* And when she sings "Believe in yourself as I believe in you," it sends chills down my arms.

Now let me tell you the phrase I *always* say when meeting with someone for the first time and explaining my approach as a therapist:

"You are the expert of you. I see myself as a guide here to help you through this process."

In my years as a counselor, I've learned that the answers people seek almost always come from within. After all, we know ourselves better than anyone else. Sometimes, of course, we need a bit of help to uncover them, which means finding the right person who believes in us until we can believe in ourselves, but the answers are there.

You can choose to continue on the path you've been on, carrying the same weight, or you can choose to take a different path, one that leads to freedom and self-understanding. The life-changing opportunity to choose to make decisions for yourself cannot be overstated. India Arie captured the idea of having a choice beautifully in her 2006 song "I Choose."—you might not know where life will take you, and you for sure cannot change where you have been in life. But today, right now, you have an opportunity. That opportunity is for you to choose.

This book—this journey, really—is about you reclaiming your power and recognizing that you have the ability to shape your own life, no matter what's happened before.

If you've been asking yourself, "What is wrong with me?" I want you to know that your reactions, your feelings, and your coping mechanisms have been your brain's and your body's courageous attempts to navigate difficult circumstances. They are not flaws but survival strategies. Making this distinction is key to shifting your perspective and discovering a path forward.

And you *can* move forward. As India Arie's lyrics remind us, while we can't change our past, we have the freedom to shape our future.

In this book, I want to take you on a journey to recognize and reclaim your expertise in your own life. My desire is for you to discover your freedom. Sweet liberation is waiting for you as you discover how to free yourself from limiting beliefs, weight of the past, and patterns that no longer serve you. This will not be easy, though. What I will need from you is to approach this book with an open mind and a curiosity to learn more about yourself, beyond what you think you already know.

This journey will require you to be brave, to face parts of yourself that might feel uncomfortable, and to challenge what you've always believed about yourself. If you are comfortable, you are not growing. My intention is to help you make sense of it all and demystify your experiences and the process of self-discovery.

This book is not about giving you all the answers; instead, it is about helping you ask the right questions and providing you with the tools to find your own answers. You've had the power all along, so now it is time to claim it.

SECTION I:
SO WHAT'S THE PROBLEM?

CHAPTER 1: FACING REALITY

*"Your willingness to look at your darkness is
what empowers you to change."*

– Iyanla Vanzant

I know, I know. It feels like the weight of the world is on your shoulders, doesn't it? The heaviness is unbearable. It's not going away, just hanging around like the remnants of an argument with your best friend. You are that close and familiar with it, and it's only getting heavier. *What is this?* you ask. Or maybe you know, but you keep ignoring and avoiding it.

I'm in so much pain, and I don't know why, you say. *I feel like I'm just stuck in a rut. I've tried this, this and this and*

I am still stuck, you say. *I feel like I have tried everything and nothing works.*

PILING ON THE WEIGHT

Imagine you are walking with a small backpack holding all of your stuff on your back. As you are walking along the flat surface, the bag feels heavy but manageable. It doesn't slow you down much.

You even start to question, well what the heck is in this bag? But you do not dare remove it. It is amazing how accustomed you have become to feeling this way. It feels almost normal. All you know is you need to keep moving no matter what, and you are willing to drag this weight to the moon and back to get to your destination.

As you start to pick up the pace and hit the incline of life, you start to feel the weight just a little differently. It may be a little hard to breathe even, but you are determined to get up that hill. Have you ever heard yourself say "I just need to push through" or "Let me just push through this one last time"?

Now, you are at the top of the incline of life. Your legs are feeling weak, and your breath shifts to panting. The backpack is truly unbearable. You are now in the thick of life. The end is often in sight, but the burden can be just too much to bear and stop you prematurely.

You can't go any further. You find yourself stumbling and making mistakes, holding yourself back from opportunities, confused, tired and dazed even. Maybe you are floating along in life, not fully present.

If this sounds familiar, then I'm talking to you. The weight piles on without you even noticing most times. It can grow little by little, inch by inch, and pound by pound. One difficult experience piled upon another, reshaping the way you think, act, and function in your day-to-day life. Most times you are pretty good at maneuvering and other times not so much. Those moments when you are, you begin to tell yourself, I'm just getting stronger, and the man upstairs won't put more on me than I can handle. Mind over matter even, and yet the burden is so heavy it hurts.

CALLING IT OUT

Acknowledging the weight you're carrying is the first step toward finding relief. I'm not talking about the pounds you see on your body. I'm actually talking about the invisible weight. It shows up in ways you may be familiar with but haven't made the connection yet. You are probably squinching your face trying to put this all together.

Here is what I am talking about: the emotional weight of your past experiences and the weight of other experiences that were passed down to you from generations past. You can be seen toting this unwanted weight as though you were the bag lady herself. You are even flaunting these weighted bags as if they were designer and have just come off the Paris runway.

By acknowledging that your burden, as it is called, is heavy, you now have taken the first step and you are aware and are not merely moving through the motions of life. You begin to ask questions of yourself, what is going on and why do I feel so heavy? You may even think to yourself, I don't want to live this way anymore, but I don't know what to do. As you begin to recognize the heaviness, you begin to take steps towards identifying it.

So, guess what? It's okay that you feel overwhelmed by it all, and it's okay to acknowledge that the burden you're carrying is heavy. This is actually where it all starts. It's so much to handle; it is so heavy. You have been weighed down for so long it now has become just a part of your everyday life. Depending on where you are in your life will determine how the weight of the baggage you are carrying is truly affecting you.

I CAN'T PUT THIS DOWN

You're carrying around so many responsibilities, and the thought of putting it all down seems impossible. I'm responsible and so many people are depending on me. It's only me and I can depend only on myself. Who is going to do all the things if I put something down? I have heard it from so many over and over again through all my years in practice. I hear myself at times saying it!

Let me tell you, really it can all be different. There is a way. This may feel scary, and in fact it is terrifying. You may think this is absurd and that there is no path toward figuring out how to do what feels beyond your abilities. The angst that comes from just trying to imagine putting even one thing down may send you into an anaphylactic shock.

You might be wondering, how does this work? "How do I even begin to put one thing down, let alone all of it?" Maybe there's a little voice inside that keeps saying, "No one will understand what I am going through" or "I just need to get through this" or the holy grail: "I have to do it all. If I don't, who will?" But here's the thing: it's not real to try and do it all; it's a facade. We have been taught a false message passed down through generations, and we don't even know it! Or maybe you do, but you would rather justify taking ownership of something when it's really not yours. The idea of doing it alone, though, is so daunting it raises my own anxiety.

GIVE IT A NAME

How can acknowledgement be the first step, you ask. What I have learned in my years of counseling is we can't change what we don't know exists. Oftentimes we underestimate the significance of putting into words what we need to conquer. Throughout this book you will learn to expand your vocabulary with words and without. What is the level of your emotional vocabulary?

As you are moving toward gaining insight and clarity, you may begin to recognize there are patterns to the challenges you're facing that leave you in a rut. While you may even have some knowledge of it, the difficulty may be in finding the word or words to call your experience. It's like trying to describe a complex emotion or an abstract concept that you can feel but struggle to articulate. You might have glimpses of understanding, moments of clarity, but finding the right words to encapsulate it all can feel like grasping at air.

Stay with me here. Expanding your vocabulary goes beyond simply finding the right words to describe your experiences; it's really about deepening your understanding and connection to yourself and then to the world around you. It's like adding new colors to your palette, which allows you to paint a richer and more nuanced picture of your life or adding more colorful chords to create a vibration that resonates with your soul.

Often words are not readily available to describe the visceral response or reaction to our current situation. Sometimes it is not the current situation but an old experience that your brain and body is remembering. The current situation is just a reminder of something in the past. By putting into words what we are experiencing, helps us create meaning and understanding of the situation.

As you embark on this journey to connect with yourself, each new word you learn becomes a tool for identification, introspection, understanding, and growth. You may uncover words with which you resonate deeply and which capture the feelings or experiences you couldn't quite articulate before. These words become bridges connecting your inner world to the outer, which will further help you communicate your thoughts and emotions with clarity.

WEIGHT OF LIFE

Life can be a beast. Full of ups and downs, and many times you can never be prepared fully. The only thing that is predictable about life is that it is unpredictable. My mother used to say to me, as her mother would say to her, "Just keep living." I had no clue what this meant as a child. In my childlike way, I thought, "duh, I know I will."

Of course, that is not what she meant, but I wouldn't figure this out until I was an adult. So what I understand "just keep living" to mean is that as you continue to grow up, you will learn all that life has to teach you. What you think you know about something you don't really know until you have had more experiences.

As we continue to live this thing called life, we are exposed to the ways of the world that are outside of our control. For example, as a child you were dependent upon the adults around you to clothe, bathe, feed, and shelter you. These are the basic needs or the first level of needs according to twentieth-century psychologist Abraham Maslow, who came up with a pyramid of the hierarchy of needs that helps us understand what drives human behavior. At the bottom level, we have *basic needs* such as food, water, and shelter. Without these, survival is impossible. Once those are met, we move to

14

the next level which is the need for *safety*, this means a stable home or a sense of financial security. The third level, we seek *love and belonging*, making connections with others, relationships, and a sense of community. Next comes self-*esteem*, which is the desire to feel valued and respected by yourself and by others. Lastly, at the top of the pyramid is *self-actualization*, the pursuit of our highest potential, creativity, and personal growth. The core belief of Maslow's idea is that we must satisfy our more basic needs before we can move on to the deeper, more fulfilling desires that shape our lives.

As you grow older and gain more ability to take care of your own needs, you may learn from the lessons of life. The lived experiences of those responsible for you were being passed down may have sometimes been for your good and sometimes to your detriment.

MOMENT OF PAUSE

Let's take a moment here to breathe. Take a deep breath in through your nose and blow all the air out through your mouth. As you continue reading you will learn how to get yourself unstuck?

You don't have to keep feeling this way, there's something you can do about this. Realizing that you're in pain and understanding where the weight of it all is coming from, leads you to naming it. Once you name it, the clouds will begin to part and now the work begins.

But first, to get started, without words you are going to just notice the environment, the space in which you occupy. You may be saying "wait huh? You just said we need the words to have understanding." Hear me out for a moment. Start by taking a deep breath through your nose and exhaling out of your mouth. Now turn your attention inward. You may begin to notice the tension in your muscles or fluttering in your heart. You may even notice a sensation of constriction in your throat, as if your words are trapped when trying to speak. This is your body communicating with you.

Your body also has its own language. It has its own way of trying to bring awareness to you and yet we often ignore its messages. Let's delve deeper into this. The experience of trauma, whether acute or compounded as a child, changes your brain and your body's nervous system, leaving you to have experiences that you just can't quite put your finger on. Maybe you have gone to multiple doctors, taken numerous blood tests, and had PET and MRI scans, and there is still no explanation as to what you are experiencing.

Imagine your brain and body as a sophisticated smartphone. I'm sure your smartphone is not far from you; you may be reading this from your phone in fact. Your phone has both hardware and software components. Your phones software is *the brain* or the operating system. It controls and coordinates all the functions. *The body* of your phone is the hardware, which houses all the components.

THE BREAKDOWN

Let's get to the nitty gritty so you can begin to understand a complex issue in a simple and relatable way: the neurobiology of the heaviness or in other words the trauma. Our brain can be considered the equivalent to the operating system within the smartphone. There are several key components of the brain that will help give clarity to some of your body's responses in relation to your past experiences.

First, we have the amygdala. You can think of the amygdala as the phone's alarm system, constantly monitoring for threats and danger. After experiencing a traumatic event the amygdala can become overactive, triggering the body's stress response and causing heightened fear and anxiety. It's like setting multiple alarms and not knowing when they will go off. To add to it all, when they go off, you can't shut them off.

Next let's explore the hippocampus. Consider the hippocampus as the phone's memory storage system. It's responsible for encoding and retrieving memories.

Experiencing a traumatic event can disrupt the hippocampus, leading to difficulties in forming and recalling memories of the traumatic event. The specific details of the traumatic event become fragmented and disjointed, making it further difficult to make sense of your past and current experiences.

The third key component is the prefrontal cortex. Imagine the prefrontal cortex as the phone's executive center, responsible for decision-making, planning, and emotional regulation. A traumatic event can cause the prefrontal cortex to shut down. When that happens, thinking through a situation and making decisions becomes null and void. When you can't control your emotions you can't control your impulses or regulate your emotions.

Like a smartphone, our nervous systems transmit signals between the brain and the body, coordinating bodily functions and responses. The traumatic event dysregulates the nervous system, which leads to symptoms such as heightened arousal, hypervigilance, and dissociation.

Then there is the hormonal system, which regulates critical bodily functions such as metabolism, growth, reproduction, stress response, and mood. Your hormones travel through the bloodstream, sending signals to cells and organs, coordinating their activities to maintain balance and respond to changes in the environment. When trauma affects the hormonal system it's equivalent to the smartphone encountering a glitch in its hardware. Traumatic events can trigger the release of stress hormones like cortisol and adrenaline, activating the body's "fight or flight" response. This response is crucial for surviving threatening situations, but chronic or intense trauma can dysregulate the hormonal system, leading to long-term physical and psychological effects.

Now imagine your immune system is like the phone's security system that protects against any viruses or infections. The experience of a traumatic event can weaken your immune system and create vulnerability to physical illnesses and health problems. Much like how a skilled technician can troubleshoot and repair a malfunctioning smartphone, a skilled therapist can support and help you heal from the effects of trauma and restore balance to your brain and body system. While this glitch may exist, there is the possibility for healing, or an opportunity for the internal software to be updated.

Through therapies like cognitive-behavioral therapy, Eye Movement Desensitization and Reprocessing

(EMDR) therapy, Internal Family Systems (IFS), mindfulness, and somatic experiencing, you can reprogram your brain's responses to trauma and rebuild resilience, allowing you to navigate life with greater ease and well-being. This is no small feat. It is hard, but you can do the hardest of things. You really can. There are three core pieces needed to do this hard work: openness, willingness, and effort. With these three things you can certainly do the hard thing. So now ask yourself:

How open am I to exploring the known and the unknown of myself?

How willing am I to commit to the process of this discovery?

What effort will it take for me to be open and willing to gain a deeper understanding of myself and my needs?

EXERCISE: ACTIVATING YOUR SENSES

Now that you understand how your brain's operating system functions, it's time to run the program. Follow these steps to explore and connect to your breath and senses.

1. **Get Comfortable**: Settle into where you are and get yourself as comfortable as possible. Find a

seat or lie down in a way that supports your body.

2. **Focus Inward**: Take a moment to focus inward, bringing your attention to your breath.

3. **Breathe** for one minute, focus solely on your breathing. Pay attention to the sensation of air entering and leaving your body.

4. **Visualize the Balloon**: As you become more attentive to your breathing, visualize a balloon filling with air.

5. **Inhale**: Breathe in through your nose, counting to three. As you do this, imagine the balloon filling with air.

6. **Hold** your breath for a count of three.

7. **Exhale** slowly, visualizing the balloon deflating. Release all the air from your lungs until there is no more.

8. **Repeat**: Continue this cycle for 3 rounds, or until you feel your body sinking into your seat.

By focusing on your breath and the balloon, you allow yourself to activate your senses and deepen your connection to your body. Continue to practice this exercise whenever you need to center yourself and activate your senses

CHAPTER 2: IT CAME FROM SOMEWHERE

*"There is no greater agony than bearing an
untold story inside you."*

— **Maya Angelou**

I went into my son's room to ensure he was completing his finals as he was wrapping up his senior year. He gave me that annoyed look like what could you possibly want now. There was a piece of paper on the edge of his bed and the words "post-traumatic stress disorder" caught my eye. I picked up the paper and read the paragraphs. It resonated in such a way because it sounded so familiar to all the stories I had heard from my clients over the years. It illustrates PTSD so well, I thought it important to share.

I am the shadow that chases you even in the night, the echo of a heartbeat in a silent room. I am the monster with a million faces, each one showcased in a video of your past that plays on repeat in your head. I ensure that the past is always your present, that your wounds never fully heal. I keep the past playing like a movie reel that is looped. I whisper in your ear, asking what if, what then, what now? The doubt that clouds your judgment, the uncertainty that darkens your days is all me.

All are welcome and no one is immune. I haunt the young and the old, the rich and the poor, the strong and the weak. I am an equal-opportunity tormentor, blind to the boundaries that typically divide HUE-man-ity. I appear in any and every form. I can be as familiar as your mother's voice, or as comforting as your father's arms only to twist those memories into something sinister. I can be as innocent as your pet waiting at the door, or as menacing as your own reflection staring back at you. I am Post

Traumatic Stress Disorder (PTSD) (Akil Creswell, 2024)

The thing about trauma is that it will make itself right at home, even when you're desperate for some peace and quiet. It is like the quiet pounding of a heartbeat in an empty room that is ever present and loud. However, it is only you that hears it constantly. You may try to silence it, but it's always there, creating a cacophony of dysregulated rhythm in the background. It is like the ghost that just doesn't quit and certainly is no Casper.

You know those moments when you feel something is wrong in your body but can't figure out what? That's where trauma lives—in the shadows of our minds and body. It is in the painful memories that show up in the middle of the night when you're staring at the ceiling unable to sleep. It's like you're trapped in a movie you never asked to watch, those scenes playing on repeat, each scene a painful reminder of what you've been through. You may be lying there numb and realizing that most of your day you haven't felt a thing. You're numb.

And just when you think you've got it figured out, that feeling shows up in ways you never saw coming. You might start to feel unsettled, always on alert, and even fearful of your own shadow. It can affect your relationships and your ability to connect and trust. It can happen to anyone, anywhere, at any time. When the traumatic event is severe and recurrent, the effects can be long lasting. They can even last a lifetime if never addressed.

How did we end up here, tangled in this mess of hurt and heartache?

HOW DID I GET HERE?

Every story has a starting point, and when it comes to trauma, for many, the experiences growing up is that starting point. The way you were treated, whether or not your needs were met, all affected who you are today.

When we talk about trauma, it's about experiences that shake us to our core, leaving a lasting impact on our lives. According to the American Psychological Association trauma is an emotional response to an event that harms or threatens harm by experiencing or witnessing an event such as sexual assault, natural disasters, childhood maltreatment, domestic violence, armed conflict, a sudden death, human trafficking and terrorism. The response to experiencing a trauma can be shock, denial, flashbacks, strained relationships, physical manifestations, and unpredictable emotions.

Trauma can also be rooted in childhood memories and experiences. You know, those old family secrets that you were told never to tell. What happens in this house stays in this house. Oh, I know you know that one. Those old family patterns of behavior that somehow got passed down like a family heirloom. Yes, those.

Finally, trauma can be exacerbated by our own actions—the things we do to try to cope with the trauma from everything else. Oh, my goodness, we get in our own way! Even if we don't intend to, engaging in self-destructive habits—such as drug use, overspending, binge eating or restricting, and maybe even risky sexual behavior—can just keep piling on the hurt. We just might inflict wounds on ourselves by not having healthy ways of coping or simply not having any ways of coping at all. Maybe we continuously strive for perfection as a way to counter the stereotypes imposed on women, which can lead to burnout and mental exhaustion. Maybe as a way to cope with the burdens of societal expectations we push ourselves to unhealthy limits.

Self-destructive beliefs often stem from childhood experiences, past relationships, and societal influences. For example, a woman might internalize the belief that she needs to work twice as hard to be seen as half as good, a sentiment rooted in both racism and sexism. These beliefs can be deeply ingrained and difficult to dismantle, especially when the experiences of that woman continue to say otherwise.

Trauma can also come from outside sources, like the expectations and rules placed on us by society.

Society certainly has a lot to say about who you are, who you should be, when you should get married, how long you should stay married. Even the number of children you should have and when you should have said children. Whew, I'm sweating!

But wait, there's more. Some in society even have the nerve to say that you, woman, and you, young girl, do not have the legal right to make decisions about your reproductive health. This may have you feeling helpless and maybe even hopeless. When the law says you can't take care of your body and keep it safe and healthy, fear sends your autonomic nervous system into fight-or-flight mode. The fear that you may not live because you can't take care of your medical needs may even cause your autonomic nervous system to freeze.

Feeling that you have no control, feeling that your life is at risk, or feeling immobilized due to the trauma, is trauma. Especially when they recreate old patterns or old experiences that have occurred over the course of your lifetime.

What is important to know is that trauma doesn't discriminate, plain and simple. It'll latch onto anyone and everyone. It doesn't care about your age, your bank account, or your social status. It's like Mayhem in the Allstate commercials who crashes in and wreaks havoc, no questions asked.

It's time to shine a light on all of it. It's not always pretty, but the truth is, whether you know it right now or not, you can do the hardest of things.

BRAIN BODY CONNECTION IN ACTION

The mere thought of digging into your past is terrifying. You have worked so hard to try and forget or compartmentalize just so you can get through the day. Everything in you says run away from the proverbial fire, but I am going to ask you to do the opposite of what seems natural. I am going to ask you to lean in.

I commend you for doing what was needed and figuring out a way to keep yourself safe and a functioning citizen of society. What often gets missed is that the memories you stuff away are stored in your body. So, while you may have figured out how to clear your mind somewhat, the effects of the trauma continue to show up and show out in your body.

Once a traumatic experience occurs, the world as you know it becomes shattered into many pieces. The memory becomes fragmented and often will emotionally overwhelm your system. Because the memories can be fuzzy and the details fragmented, it is often like trying to put together a puzzle with half the pieces missing. This makes it nearly impossible to actually have a complete picture or story, which makes it difficult to heal. The memory of the event may come back in bits and pieces, in other words as flashbacks and body sensations, aches and pains, along with intense dysregulated emotions.

These are the experiences that you may find difficult to explain to your primary care physician; you just know you feel it. They run all the tests and do all the bloodwork, a complete workup, but everything comes back normal, leaving you further disillusioned. It is so frustrating and upsetting when you have very real physical aches and pains and inflammation, yet it can't be explained medically. Heart palpitations that feel like a heart attack but can't be explained medically could mean your body is remembering. Our bodies carry all the designer bags. Once this connection is made, there is a pathway to healing, to releasing those heavy "designer bags" of trauma.

The automation of your brain and body is beautiful and amazing. It is imperative to grasp the intricate connection between trauma and your body's responses in order to gain understanding of your experiences through your nervous system. The polyvagal theory, developed by Dr. Stephen Porges, provides a scientific explanation of your nervous system's response to stress and trauma.

Stay with me as I parse out a different understanding for the brain body experience. Our autonomic nervous system (ANS) plays a crucial role in how we react to traumatic events. Our ANS is made up of three parts: the ventral vagal, the sympathetic nervous system (SNS), and the dorsal vagal (DV). Each one of these parts influences our emotional and physiological states, guiding our responses to safety and danger.

The ventral vagal, or the social engagement system, helps us feel safe and connected to others. This is the optimal state and oftentimes can be difficult to maintain once it is reached. When this system is active, we're able to engage socially, feel calm, communicate openly, and experience positive emotions.

When a threat is perceived, however, the sympathetic nervous system kicks in, triggering what you certainly may have heard of before called the "fight or flight" response. This is our body's way of gearing up to either meet the danger head on or escape it. If the threat persists or becomes overwhelming, the dorsal vagal may take over, leading you to a freeze response. This immobilization is a protective mechanism, but it can also leave us feeling numb, disconnected, and stuck, much like carrying those heavy "designer bags" of trauma.

When we experience trauma, it can disrupt the normal functioning of these systems, causing us to become stuck in a heightened state of arousal, which can result in physical symptoms (SNS dominance), such as a racing heart, rapid breathing, muscle tension, and difficulties with sleep. Your body is on high alert, constantly scanning for potential threats, even when none are present.

The other end of the spectrum of experience is a state of low energy or emotional shutdown (DV dominance). In this state, the body and mind are in a kind of protective mode where everything slows down, and you might feel numb, disconnected, or detached from your surroundings. This emotional shutdown can manifest as fatigue, a sense of emptiness, difficulty concentrating, and a lack of emotional response. You may feel as though you are moving through life in slow motion, unable to fully experience or connect with what's happening around you.

This dysregulation explains why you might feel numb, anxious, or disconnected long after the traumatic event has passed. It's as if your body is constantly on high alert or shutdown, anticipating danger even in safe situations. This chronic state of dysregulation can manifest through physical symptoms or emotional distress—which can cause difficulties in relationships—as our nervous system struggles to find balance.

HEALING IS POSSIBLE

There is a way to heal from these experiences. The process of healing through trauma requires actively engaging in practices that promote self-regulation, safety, and connection, both within yourself and with others.

One of the foundational steps in this healing process is to establish a sense of safety, both externally and internally. Creating a safe environment can mean surrounding yourself with supportive people, engaging in activities that bring joy and calm, and removing yourself from harmful situations whenever possible. This may be simple for some people, but for others it's not so easy.

By understanding and working with your body's natural responses, you can begin to release the grip of trauma. There are exercises you can do that can help soothe the nervous system and nurture a sense of internal security. Techniques such as mindfulness, reiki, and therapies such as EMDR, which can help you desensitize old, unwanted memories and regulate your nervous system to reach a state of calm and safety.

Being able to focus on the present moment and observing your thoughts and feelings without judgment is key to healing. You can create a buffer between your triggers and your responses with the use of tools such as breathing exercises and meditation. These are powerful skills to have for your toolbox on this journey to healing. Those practices help activate the ventral vagal, which encourages a state of calm and connection.

Deep breathing exercises can directly influence your autonomic nervous system. *You want me to just breathe?* you might be thinking. But it's not *just* breathing. Intentional breathing can change your entire world. Slow, deep breaths can stimulate the vagus nerve, which will promote relaxation and help to shift you from a heightened state of arousal to one of tranquility.

Physical activities such as yoga, Pilates, and other forms of gentle exercise also play a crucial role in regulating your nervous system. Gentle exercises not only help you to release physical tension, but they also enhance your body awareness, allowing you to tune into your internal states and respond with greater resilience. When you are engaging in regular physical activity it can help rewire your nervous system, promoting a balanced state that is neither heightened nor under aroused.

As you begin to learn to navigate your internal landscape, you can start to unpack those "designer bags," freeing yourself from the weight of past trauma and ushering in a healthier, more connected you.

You are in control! You have the power to change your internal experience. I want to just remind you that you are in the here and now. You are more capable now than you may ever have been.

THE WORK YOU MUST DO

Recovering from trauma is not a passive process; it calls for you to make intentional effort and a commitment to your healing journey. Healing from trauma requires some work. Here is what you can do. Find a directory of therapists in your area (see the Resources page) and locate someone who provides therapeutic approaches designed to do the deep work, ones specifically designed to address trauma stored in the body. These include EMDR, Internal Family Systems (IFS), somatic experiencing, and sensorimotor psychotherapy.

These therapies work to help you process traumatic memories in a way that integrates both your way of thinking and bodily experiences. EMDR, for instance, uses bilateral stimulation (which is moving your eyes side to side rapidly) or butterfly tapping to help reprocess traumatic memories. While it doesn't make the memories go away, it will reduce their emotional charge. Somatic experiencing focuses on releasing the physical tension that is associated with the traumatic event. Sensorimotor psychotherapy combines talk therapy with physical interventions to address the body's role in trauma.

As you embark on this journey, breathe deeply and be aware of your internal and external environment. What we understand is that trauma embeds itself in the mind and body, often producing physical symptoms and emotional turmoil. Your healing will involve confronting these memories and understanding the brain-body connection. Utilizing techniques like mindfulness, breathing exercises, and therapies such as EMDR and IFS will place you on the path to recovery. The goal is to establish safety, reconnect with yourself, and gradually unpack the burdens of past trauma to create a future you could only imagine before now.

EXERCISE: SENSORIMOTOR INTEGRATION
FOR TRAUMA HEALING

This exercise will help to build awareness of your
mind-body connection, promote a sense of safety and
grounding that is essential for healing from trauma.

1. **Setting the Stage**
   o Find a quiet, comfortable place where you
     won't be disturbed.
   o Wear loose, comfortable clothing.
   o Have a yoga mat or a soft surface to lie
     down on.

2. **Grounding Exercise**
   o Sit or lie down comfortably.
   o Take a few deep breaths, inhaling through
     your nose and exhaling through your mouth.
   o Feel the support of the ground beneath
     you. Imagine roots growing from your
     body into the earth, grounding you.

3. **Body Scan**
   o Close your eyes and take a few moments to
     tune into your body.
   o Starting from the top of your head, slowly
     move your attention down to your toes.

o Notice any areas of tension, discomfort, or numbness. Don't try to change anything, just notice.

4. **Breath Awareness**

   o Place one hand on your abdomen and breathe from your diaphragm.

   o Practice diaphragmatic breathing: Inhale deeply so that your abdomen rises more than your chest, then exhale slowly.

   o Notice the rise and fall of your breath.

5. **Gentle Movement**

   o Begin with small, gentle movements such as shoulder rolls, neck stretches, and ankle rotations.

   o Pay attention to any sensations in your body as you move. Move in ways that feel soothing and natural to you.

6. **Vagal Breathing**

   o Sit comfortably with a straight spine.

   o Inhale deeply for a count of four, hold for a count of four, exhale for a count of six, and pause for a count of two.

   o Repeat for five minutes, focusing on the sensation of your breath and the calming effect on your body.

7. **Mindful Touch**

   o Use your hands to gently tap different parts of your body, starting with your arms, then moving to your legs, back, and torso.

   o Notice the sensation of your touch and any changes in your body's tension or relaxation.

8. **Closing**

   o End the exercise with a few deep breaths.

   o Express gratitude to yourself for taking this time to connect with your body and mind.

   o When you're ready, gently bring your awareness back to the room and open your eyes.

   o After the exercise, take a few moments to write down any sensations, emotions, or thoughts that arose during the practice.

   o Reflect on any insights or connections you made between your physical sensations and your emotional state.

SECTION 2:
GET UNSTUCK BY BALANCING EXPECTATIONS, NEEDS, WANTS & INTENTIONS

CHAPTER 3: YOU WANT ME TO DO WHAT?

"Gonna lay down my burden / Down by the riverside / Down by the riverside / Down by the riverside / Gonna lay down my burden / Down by the riverside / I ain't gonna study war no more / Study war no more / Ain't gonna study war no more."

—African-American spiritual

What is a burden you ask? What does it mean to lay down my burdens? Well, often, as women we feel compelled to continue to go beyond our limits. In fact, the trope is that it is a good thing to push yourself until you have no more in you. That means you have given your all and done everything you can. In other words, you're *really* doing good when you don't set limits, when you live in "go mode."

I hear some version of this on a daily basis: "If I just help this one additional person," "I have to take it all on because it is just me," "this is what I am supposed to do," or " I have to give 100 percent." Here are some of the best ones yet: "Well, they need me" and "Wouldn't you want someone to do this for you?" And the head banger: "They expect me to do it all."

Do you feel seen yet? Many may even say *What's the problem here; it is what it is.* I'm going to challenge you here for a minute. Just bear with me and hear me out.

While any or all of the above statements may be true, they are not the only truth. So how do we discover the *rest* of the truth? By asking ourselves questions like these:

"What if I didn't take it all on and I delegated some tasks to others?"

"What if I gave 75 percent and saved 25 percent to recover from going and going?"

"What if I took a long, honest look at all the things I believe are my responsibility? What if I discovered that some of the burdens I carry really belong to someone else, and I am not responsible at all?"

Let's take a look at where some of the expectations come from.

HAND-ME-DOWN EXPECTATIONS

As you begin to look closely at the heavy "designer bags" you've been lugging around, you may realize that some of them were given to you by past generations. The ways you have learned have gotten you this far, and it's good that you have worked so hard to figure out a pathway to safety. The messages and teachings that are passed down from past generations and through family, friends, and society, and our current position within the intersection of who we are, all provide guidance and direction for living life. It's not always helpful, and not even healthy in most cases, but a message is as a message does. Or in this instance, a burden passed down is as a burden passed down does.

Legacy burdens are the emotional and psychological weights passed down through generations. Those legacy burdens can show up as family expecting you to remain living in the same town as the rest of the family, although you may have career opportunities elsewhere, or pressures to perform academically and financially in spite of your mental health needs. Each placing a significant strain on you.

For instance, as a woman of color I can tell you that a common message that mothers pass down to their daughters is to overwork ourselves to prove that we are a valuable asset, particularly in spaces dominated by white men. Be strong, but not too strong or you may be considered a threat. Be nurturing and provide a soft-landing for your spouse and children, but don't spend too much time there because you need to be hard and strong to protect yourself.

For women of color—and, in fact, for most women—there is an expectation passed down through the generations to care for the emotional needs of your family and friends alike at the expense of caring for our own emotional needs. When would you do that? When you are expected to care for others, caring for yourself becomes just another thing to do, and something that is much easier to skip doing.

Are you seeing the designer bags come and land on your front porch now?

These legacy burdens can manifest as beliefs or behaviors ingrained in you by your family, culture, and communities. When you begin to understand the legacy of burdens, you begin to recognize that some burdens may not be yours to carry and that it's okay to question and release them.

Statements that often accompany legacy burdens include "It's just the way it has always been." Have you ever heard that before?

Or maybe you hear yourself saying things like, "I just feel heavy, and I don't know why," "I was always told to do this thing," or "I don't even know why I need to do this."

When you find yourself saying these things, it's time to recognize that the burden is *not* yours to carry!

SOCIETY'S EXPECTATIONS: TALE OF TWO WORLDS

We tend to underestimate the expectations that society places on women as a whole and particularly women of color. In general, women face a plethora of societal expectations. As women of color, however, navigating the world and societal expectations has its own set of challenges and an extra set of societal burdens.

Oftentimes women of color experience these pressures with intensity due to the additional layer of racial stereotypes and discrimination. Yes, as far as we have come, it is unbelievable that we are still working to overcome the stereotypes and discrimination that women of color face in the media.

The "strong Black woman" trope demands that Black women appear resilient and self-sufficient at all times, leaving little to no room for vulnerability or for seeking help. Due to this expectation of strength coupled with the stigma surrounding mental health difficulties, many women of color forgo seeking help to address mental health concerns. This perceived strength continues to cause problems within the healthcare system. There is a perception that black women feel less pain or no pain, leading to a high maternal death rate for black women.

Dr. Kimberly Crenshaw introduced the concept of intersectionality to help identify the multiple forms of inequality and obstacles experienced by women of color. As an example, the intersection in which I sit is at the crossroads of being" an educated woman of color, a wife, a mother that has a daughter and a son, a daughter, sister, friend, niece, aunt and a business owner. When I look through this lens, on paper it sounds as though all should be right with the world. However, as it stands, trying to balance all these roles and live up to the expectations other people have of me in my roles along with the expectations that I have of myself becomes overwhelming! We will talk more about this in the coming chapters. But gee whiz can a sister cut herself some slack? Nope!

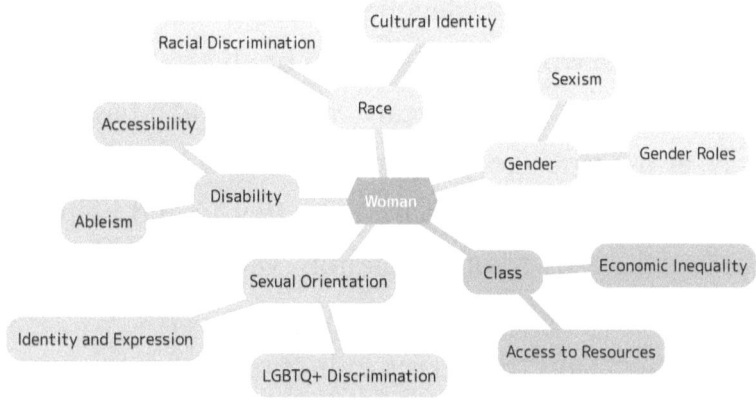

So where are you within the intersection? Women as a whole are constantly bombarded by conflicting messages, and the goal post is always moving. This makes it nearly impossible to ever feel as though we are getting ahead or that there is forward movement.

For example, we are expected to be beautiful according to the ever-changing standards of our society, leaving us to question what beauty these days is, especially when we don't see anyone who looks like us.

We are told to get an education, but when we do we are told that we are overqualified for the jobs that are available to us.

Even in 2024, as women we have fewer rights than our foremothers, although we have more than their mothers. I don't know if that is a thing, but I wanted to crack a smirk for a moment because this is so unbelievably frustrating and truthfully sad.

To top it all off, depending on the state in which you live, as a woman you may not be able to receive certain reproductive healthcare. If some folks have their way, at the ripe age of ripeness you may not be able to benefit from medical technology that would help you further the growth of your family, yet you are expected to have a family.

Society says I am to reproduce to further the agenda of family, yet if for some reason my body is working against me, I can't receive the treatment that I would need to have said children. Society says, I am to stay at home and take care of my home and my children, yet I can't afford to live without working to take care of said family. If I seek assistance in order to do as expected of me, I am told I need to pull myself up by the bootstraps and get a job. Okay, I hear you, society. So I go get a job, but now I need childcare! When society says no assistance for childcare, what I make in a paycheck goes to childcare. But then when I put my children in daycare, society says that I'm being neglectful and shouldn't send my children to be taken care of by someone else. That I should stay home and do it myself. Do you hear the insanity in all of this? This is the message! Talk about mixed messaging, confusing, draconian, and whatever else you would want to call it.

Talk about a burden. Whew, child! What do you want from us society?

As a woman who struggled to have her children and had to seek IVF treatment to have a family, I understand from a firsthand point of view of the struggle. This leaves me to think about where we are currently, and it is quite frightening.

It creates the familiar feeling that the experience of a traumatic event brings about, helplessness and hopelessness. Society is perpetuating the traumatic experience of it all, by not being good stewards of its women.

I'm not here to convince you of anything. Instead, I'm here to challenge your thinking toward societal expectations. Recognizing that you have choice and able to focus on your needs, desires, and healing is a way to take back power in your life. Surround yourself with people and the transformational therapies will assist you to get there. Having choices can be terrifying when it has been missing for long periods. Once you realize you have power, wholeheartedly embrace your ability to choose the way you will live from this day forward, the song by the group Black Sheep begins to play in my head, "The Choice is Yours." The choice truly is yours.

FAMILY EXPECTATIONS

Family is tricky. The relationships and dynamics are not always like the Brady Bunch or even the Huxtables. Maybe you don't have a connection to your biological family, but you have created a family with the people around you. Regardless of the relationship and no matter how the family was created, there are expectations that family members have of one another. They may or may not be spoken, but there is an understanding of your role and how your family sees you in it.

Like society at large, each family has a culture, and within that, you have learned how to navigate that world just as you navigate the world around you. As you have received messages passed down from generations, you most likely have taken in the messages that serve you well and thrown out ones that have a negative influence. Then there are those messages of expectations that found a way to seep deep down into your system that wreak havoc, messages such as, *you must do for others even if they don't show up for you.* These messages often end up convincing you to do all the things for everyone but yourself, leaving you depleted.

You are selfish to put yourself first, they say. Now that we are trying to take back the word *selfish* and own it as a good thing, your brain can't quite compute—nor shake the guilt that pours over your being for doing something for yourself. Let's see what this looks like for you: What was supposed to be an entire day of pampering becomes half a day, and instead you take the second half of the day taking care of other people's needs. Is this you?

Look, girlfriend, I'm not trying to call you out. I'm just sayin'. It is all about awareness. We can't change anything if we can't see it. Have you ever tried to change something that you couldn't see? Impossible! We become aware of something through our sensory perception, or in other words our brain interprets and comprehends the information received through our senses—sight, hearing, touch, taste, and smell.

Our brains process these environmental sensory inputs using language to label and categorize the stimuli, thereby creating understanding and communication. It is language that will enable us to make sense of the world around us. As van der kolk (2014) states, "We have discovered that helping victims of trauma find the words to describe what has happened to them is profoundly meaningful".... p.21 If we can't name what we experienced that has affected us, then it becomes difficult to make sense of our response and to communicate to others our emotional status. And we can't make any changes.

It's not just you, but me as well. My family also has expectations of me in ways that I was not fully aware. I thought I had an idea of how people in my family saw me, but rather than go by my own thoughts, I took a poll to find out how my family actually experienced me and what they expected of me. What I thought I knew, I actually didn't. The responses to a question I posed were surprising to say the least. Yes, they did expect a lot of me. Some of the expectations I already sensed; others were news to me. But what was really affirming to me in doing this exercise was the acknowledgement and appreciation the family felt for what I gave to them.

Here is the question I posed and the responses I received:

How do you see me or experience me within our family system and what expectations do you have of me?

1. Personally, I see you as an aunt even though we're technically cousins. As far as expectations, I expect to be my authentic self around you while I also expect you to be your authentic self around me with all the honesty that comes with it.

2. I see you as someone who values authenticity and connection within our family. I have come to expect meaningful conversations and

gestures of care from you, such as remembering to wish me happy birthday.

3. I see you as my anchor and also the family. You are the go-to person for support and understating. Since you possess all of these qualities, we EXPECT for you to show up for us and help us sort out our mess and don't stop to think you are dealing with your own mess. Because sometimes you make it look easy.

4. I see you as a dear younger cousin who has grown into a dynamic and capable woman. I see you as an amazing mother, daughter and spouse. I see you as a friend and confidant.

5. I see you as a crucial guiding figure within our family. Your experiences and wisdom have been invaluable to me. I don't expect anything specific from you on a daily basis, but I have a deep-seated confidence in your willingness to help when needed. I do so with the expectation that you'll come through for me.

6. I don't have many expectations from you. I would just hope you reach out to me if you need me, and I would hope that I can reach out to you if I need you. I also expect that you be honest with me and call me out if I'm not doing what I'm supposed to.

7. I see you as the leader, quiet but like the inspector.... Also a trend setter..... Also as my little sister, even though you're only three months younger, but I've always looked out for you as you have for me all these years. I appreciate you!

There was more grace and understanding from my family than I give to myself. Here I had been thinking my family had so many expectations of me that they wouldn't understand if I took time to take care of myself. Boy, was I wrong!

8. I see you from a state of Love, unconditional love! Now, what I expect of you is to give you more U&U time! Connect more with God already in You and YOU! For YOU, take every day, a fifteen-minute moment of silence for you, for your mind, body and soul. Nobody is allowed in that fifteen minutes.

9. I see you/experience you as one of the voices of reason in our family.... I feel like you are one of the level-headed voices that comes out of that. I also experience you as being kind and funny and just overall having great energy about you. My expectations of you are to continue being you but don't spread yourself too thin.

What am I to take from this? Well, the role I have, whether it was given to me or I somehow picked it out of the family role aisle at Target, is the authentic anchor of connection. I am the go-to person, a problem solver or voice of reason, and I somehow make it all look easy. That is my burden; those are my designer bags that I carry. I also gained new awareness and further understanding of myself through the eyes of my family.

What might this mean for you? Just take a moment and think about what your role is within your own family constellation and what the expectations they may have of you. This exercise was meant to offer a way for you to gain awareness and further understanding of yourself.

MOVING FORWARD

Even though I am a therapist, I am human and have my own designer bags. As a therapist, I am trained to set my designer bags off to the side, so they are not a distraction as I seek to help you with yours. But trust me when I say they are close enough for me to have a very real understanding of what you are going through.

Recognizing the burdens and designer bags you are carrying is the first step toward healing. It's crucial to become clear on the expectations of society to begin dismantling these burdens. Understanding that these burdens are not ours alone to bear—and that we have the power to redefine our narratives—is empowering. It allows us to break free from the chains of legacy burdens, heal from self-inflicted wounds, and build a future where we can thrive authentically.

What society and your family needs and wants from you they may not get and that is okay. It really is okay. I am here to tell you that you owe society and your family nothing more than to take good care of yourself and be the best human being you can be, and that is it. That is your assignment.

Your mental health is health care. Allowing yourself to step into what may be unfamiliar, such as the therapeutic space that can provide you a safe and objective space to unpack these issues and learn what bags you need to put down, can be difficult. It's very possible that the therapeutic space is familiar to you, but you didn't like it or didn't feel it was helpful. I encourage you to explore it once again and be empowered to know that you can search for what feels like a good fit. Ask if you can have a consultation to make this determination before jumping all in; most therapists will offer this for free. Just know that you are the expert of you, and your task will be to search for a therapist that has that same understanding. You have a say in what is happening in your life, and a therapist that includes you in the process is what creates a successful experience.

EXERCISE: REFLECTING ON SOCIETAL EXPECTATIONS

1. **Find a quiet** place and focus your attention.
2. **Reflect & List:** Consider the expectations society has placed on you in various aspects of your life (e.g., career, friendships, family). Write down these societal expectations.
3. **Identify Burdens:** Note any burdens or pressures you feel as a result of these expectations.
4. **Ask the Question**: Take a poll with your family members that you feel safe with and ask, "How do you see me or experience me within our family system, and what expectations do you have of me?"

Take your time with this exercise, and be honest with yourself about how these expectations impact you. Write your thoughts in your journal.

CHAPTER 4: ALL ABOUT YOU

*"Caring for myself is not self-indulgence,
it is self-preservation, and that is an act of
political warfare".*

— Audre Lorde

"I have to get this right and make it perfect. All I need to do is to make it to the end of it."

When was the last time you said this to yourself or someone else?

Or what about this one: "It's not fair for me to fix my own stuff before doing something for my children [partner, mother]. That would be selfish."

Now, I am here to tell you, It's not about being perfect or being selfish. Really, it's not. You know what comes at the end? You come out bruised and battered and like a piece of string cheese, just stretched and loosey goosey, destabilized, tired, and worn out.

I hear this so much, and I always sit back thinking, there has to be a different way. Why do we do this? I'm not being judgmental, because I truly understand; I have done it! It's double the stress, double the pain, and double the bruising. Far less ground gets covered and not much changes, if anything. If that is what it's about, I don't want it. Been there and done that.

PUT YOUR OXYGEN ON FIRST

Undoubtedly, you've heard flight attendants give these instructions to adults flying with kids: "If we get into trouble and oxygen masks drop from the ceiling, put your mask on first before you help your child."

Say what? Talk about counterintuitive! And how *selfish*, right? Well, if that's the word that comes to your mind, then yes, you want and need to be selfish.

And here's why.

The airplane mask example epitomizes the truth that you must first protect yourself in order to have the strength and awareness to help those you love. After all, if you collapse on the floor of the cabin, what good is that doing you or anyone else?

I get that there are times when you will want or need to put other people's needs before your own. But if you don't come back into balance, if you neglect our own needs for years, it can have a physical effect on your body. You may find yourself going to the doctor more often. They might run a battery of tests and blood work that may or may not reveal health problems, but either way, you certainly don't feel normal. This is frustrating because you know what you know, and you know you don't feel good and haven't for some time.

The health problems from the years of neglecting your well-being might look like migraines, irritable bowel syndrome, heart palpitations, weight gain or loss, and even inflammation throughout your body. The possibilities are many. The potential causes are many, too, but as science and research increasingly shows a bigger factor than we ever realized: the simple fact that we never got back to finding balance, never returned to making our emotional needs a priority. And now we are paying a heavy price. According to world renowned trauma therapist Dr. Bessel van der Kolk and author of *The Body Keeps the Score* "trauma is not just an event that took place sometime in the past; it is also the imprint left by that experience on mind, brain, and body. This imprint has ongoing consequences for how the human organism manages to survive in the present."

STOP DEFERRING YOUR DREAMS

What happens when a dream is deferred? That is the question Langston Hughes posed many moons ago, and it leaves me wondering. What really happens? Does it actually dry up and turn into a raisin? While raisins tend to be sweet, the grape is no longer in its original form. It literally turns into something else with a different name. It takes on a new image and form and no longer looks like itself.

Does it fester and become a sore spot, something you don't talk about and resent anyone who does? Does this sound familiar? No one better dare bring up the old stuff. Does it linger around until it spoils, smelling to the high heavens? It smells so bad that it takes your breath away.

Does your dream deferred give you a boost to continue working toward your goal to succeed. Does it drive you to make it happen? Or does it become this heaviness that drags you down and keeps you stuck, leaving no room for moving forward. It could be something that just blows you out of the water. What is the price to be paid to push my dreams so far back that they nearly don't exist?

While watching the hit TV show *Master Chef*, a sixty-three-year-old woman from the baby boomer generation said being there for the auditions was the first time she has done anything that was strictly for herself. Her desire only. Talk about a dream deferred. Wow! I don't know about you, but I was scared straight. I began to wonder what her life had been like up until that point. What were the stories she had been told that made deferring her own dreams and desires okay or maybe even a necessity? What had her family and society imposed on her that it was only now that she could explore her dreams for herself?

The years that have gone by, that you can't get back, only to now honor her true desire. It certainly was a teachable moment. There was no shade to this woman who was finally living out her dream. Better late than never, but it is a wake-up call to us all to reflect on where we are and consider where we want to be. The old adage of it is never too late certainly still rings true.

Sacrifice they say. To be a parent is to sacrifice. To be a caregiver is to sacrifice. To be a leader in your work is to sacrifice. To be a woman, especially a woman of color is to sacrifice. To that I say yes and no. Have

I sacrificed a thing or two? A resounding yes. Have I gotten caught up in the old messaging passed down? Absolutely, for sure. How did I know something was off? Well, when I found myself frustrated, bored, unfocused, or not remembering what happened in my day.

It is never too late to realize that the old messages that have been passed down, are no longer serving you. It is never too late to change your narrative and rewrite the way that you will live, for yourself. It is never too late to decide to send down through the generations a new message, a new way of being and doing things. It is okay to let go of the baggage. It is not yours and you can free yourself and release the weight.

LOVE ON YOURSELF

When you prioritize and honor your own needs and desires first, you set off a powerful trickle-down effect that positively impacts every area of your life. By attending to your own well-being, you are not merely indulging in self-care, you are actively cultivating the energy and capacity required to be present and supportive for others in your life. This self-attention creates a ripple effect, enhancing your overall happiness and health, which, in turn, affects how you interact with those around you. It pays to take care of you.

Stick with me for a moment. Just imagine this scenario, a parent who gets regular exercise and enough sleep finds themselves more energized and focused at work, which improves their productivity. At home, they are more patient with and attentive to their children because they aren't drained or irritable from lack of caring for themselves. Doing so creates a shift in their well-being and transforms their interactions with their family.

When you take care of your physical, emotional, and psychological needs, you foster a sense of balance and contentment within yourself. When there is inner harmony, there is room for transforming how you show up in your relationships and interactions. When you take care of yourself, you also teach the loved ones around you a different way of doing things, which changes the generational view and understanding of how we are to treat ourselves. You become more engaged, less frazzled, and more attuned to the needs of others. Those around you experience you in a new light. They encounter a version of you who is healthier, kinder, and less burdened by frustration or exhaustion. This shift in your demeanor and energy alters the dynamics of your relationships, creating a more positive and supportive environment.

With this in mind, let's consider how this dynamic can change the workplace. Can you imagine a manager who takes time for regular personal reflection and stress management. When they're feeling centered and calm, their communication with their team is more empathetic and effective. They're able to offer constructive feedback rather than reacting out of frustration. As a result, their team members feel valued and understood, leading to improved morale and productivity. This creates a win-win situation and sets a clear justification path for moving yourself in front of the line.

Oftentimes I hear all the reasons for the need to take care of others first. That there is a responsibility to certain individuals, such as your children or spouse, to ensure that all their needs are met first. Is this one of those expectations that have been passed down to you that you must do for all those before you? Well, I say no! It is never okay to put others, even your children, before yourself.

The idea of a hierarchy in which your needs are consistently deferred to the needs of others is really counterproductive. If we view the act of caring as hierarchical, and put others' needs above ours, even if only for a season, do your needs ever make it to the front again? I think it is fair to say not for a very long time, if at all. Now, I want to ask you. What is your expectation for yourself? It is very important to become clear and recognize what may be driving your decision making.

When you place yourself at the bottom of the priority list, you end up perpetuating this cycle where your needs remain unmet. This leads to a scenario where you are perpetually running on empty, leaving your own well-being neglected and can't figure out how you got here. By the time you attempt to address your needs, exhaustion has set in, and the "I'll get to me later" cycle repeats itself. In this cycle you are constantly playing catch-up, with your self-care continuously being postponed until no set time in the future.

Picture a caregiver who consistently puts their own needs last to tend to the needs of a loved one. Over time, they become increasingly overwhelmed and fatigued. Their own health deteriorates, leading to increased stress and frustration. Eventually, their diminished well-being affects their ability to provide care effectively or even in a loving way. This more than likely goes against what their original intention had been in the first place. Now they are in a cycle where both the needs of the caregiver and their loved one suffer. As a caregiver myself I know this to be true. Being a caregiver is extremely hard for a plethora of reasons, and it is easy to lose yourself in trying to do right by your loved one. I struggled when thrusted into such a role; it tripped me up. I stumbled and fell a few times before finding my way. It was all so new. I had to learn about things that most likely wouldn't affect me until twenty or thirty years later. I did what you are probably doing. I told myself I would get back to taking care of my needs in a bit, which turned into a while and then I just totally forgot. My health was paying the price, and it became clear that if I didn't take care of what my brain and my body required, I wouldn't be able to meet the needs of the people I love.

Instead of operating in this perpetual default mode, where you place everyone else's needs above your own, it is necessary for you to strive for a more balanced approach. It is important for you to intentionally evaluate your situation and find equilibrium between meeting your needs and meeting the needs of those around you. When you recognize and understand the gaps between your well-being and your obligations to others, you will be able to avoid the common pitfall of neglecting yourself.

You do not have to choose between your needs and the needs of others. It is entirely possible—and often beneficial—to address both simultaneously. By integrating self-care into your daily routine, you ensure that you are consistently on the list of priorities. Taking care of yourself enables you to be more effective and supportive in fulfilling the needs of others. In essence, when you choose yourself and your well-being, you are not just doing something for yourself; you are enhancing your capacity to contribute positively to the lives of those you care about.

Honoring your own needs doesn't have to be some far-fetched, unattainable dream. Instead, prioritizing self-care will foster greater happiness, health, and balance, which will transform how you engage with those around you. Moving away from a hierarchy that places your needs at the bottom helps prevent burnout and sets you up for a more balanced life. Integrating your self-care into your daily routine allows you to address both your needs and the needs of others simultaneously. Choosing to honor your own needs is not a selfish act but a crucial step toward fostering healthier, more fulfilling relationships and interactions with the loved ones in your life.

FOUR QUESTIONS

There are four big questions you need to ask yourself: What do I want? What do I need? What do I expect from myself and others? Lastly, What are my intentions?"

"What do I want?"
The toughest one to tackle is often, "What do I want?" This question can really throw you for a loop, especially if you're not used to having or getting what you desire, or if you've never felt allowed to voice your wants. Many times I hear people say, I don't have any wants or I don't know what I want. I challenge you to stretch yourself into this unfamiliar territory and sit with this question for a bit.

You're in it, and this process requires some deep self-exploration to come up with an honest answer. Knowing what you want straightens up all the zigzags and gives you a direct path toward a goal. When you understand what you want you can begin creating the steps to achieve your goal. Understanding your desires gives you direction and purpose, making it easier to prioritize actions that truly matter to you. This clarity not only guides your actions but also fuels your motivation and determination, connecting you to your deeper passions and aspirations.

"What do I need?"

To explore your needs is pivotal and different from identifying your wants, yet they hold equal importance. Knowing your needs helps you recognize what's essential for your well-being and continued growth. Needs really are the foundational elements, such as emotional support, financial stability, and physical health, that will sustain you. By pinpointing these needs, you are making sure that you are not neglecting the core aspects of your life that keep you grounded and fulfilled.

Once you become more self-aware, you'll be able to communicate better with others about what you require and need to feel secure and supported. Yes, you heard me correctly. You can require things. Taking care of your needs helps you avoid burnout, improves your overall well-being, boosts your productivity, and brings balance in your life. Not to mention, understanding your needs helps you set priorities that protect your mental and physical health, making you more resilient and content. It also helps you to establish boundaries when it comes to specific people in your life and by letting you know what your limits are in general. Knowing your needs empowers you to make decisions that align with your well-being, reinforcing your ability to thrive in various aspects of your life.

"What do I expect from myself and from others?"

Now let's talk about your expectations of yourself and others. Expectations have the ability to shape your relationships and impact your sense of satisfaction and disappointment. Your expectations are always there whether you know it or not. Setting realistic expectations allows you to cultivate healthier and more compassionate interactions with yourself and with other people in your life. Having this introspection will help you align your actions with your values and lead you to more meaningful connections and deeper understanding of your boundaries.

Clear expectations also build trust and mutual respect, which will further enhance the quality of your relationships. When you understand your expectations, you can communicate them more effectively, avoid misunderstandings and foster mutual respect. The more you understand your own expectation, the greater chance you have to experience a supportive environment where everyone knows their roles and responsibilities, leaving room for an environment where everyone feels heard and valued.

It is so important to manage your expectations; it is a must. By doing so, you will be able to maintain a positive self-image and avoid the disappointment that comes from having unrealistic standards that you may not have realized were present. Knowing what you expect of yourself and others is a game changer. Anytime you can have a healthier and more balanced perspective on life, you are winning and leaning into freedom.

"What are my intentions?"
Lastly, knowing your intentions brings everything into focus. It is the thread that weaves the four questions into a cohesive whole. So, let's think of your intentions as the driving force behind your actions and decisions; it is the motor. When you take time to understand your core motivations and values, and clarify your intentions, you build a strong foundation that naturally guides your actions and interactions with others.

Your intentions help you stay focused and committed to your goals, even if you should be faced with obstacles and distractions. They also enhance your ability to communicate effectively with others. Having a clear understanding of where you are coming from and the points that you want to get across, along with how you want to say them, will remove any fear of how you may be perceived by others. When you know your intentions, it helps you create and articulate your purpose and motivations with confidence.

It is necessary to have clear intentions in order to cultivate trust and alignment within your relationships. This will allow others to understand and feel your genuineness. Furthermore, having clarity of your intentions allows you to evaluate your progress and make adjustments as they are needed.

In order to have awareness of yourself, you must stop to hear yourself and see yourself as you are showing up in the world. By checking in with yourself it ensures that your actions remain consistent with your desired outcomes. In essence, your clear intentions serve as a beacon of light that will shine and lead you on your path. It will empower you to navigate the complexities of life with great purpose and integrity. When you are true to yourself, you keep it real.

I encourage you to sit and reflect on your why. It's not just about knowing what you want to achieve but also understanding why you want to achieve it. Having this deeper level of awareness will serve as a guide and ensure you will be able to align your actions with your core values. You will be less likely to be swayed by short-term distractions or superficial desires. Intentions are a constant reminder of the bigger picture, helping you maintain focus and perseverance.

The experience of a traumatic event disrupts your ability to connect to the people and the world around you. Clear intentions provide a guidepost for you to create stronger, more meaningful connections with others. When you communicate your intentions transparently, you invite others to understand your motivations and align their support with your goals.

Whew! That is powerful! You have the power to create openness, trust, collaboration, and connection. Yes, you have it; it is built in. You come into the world with this tool. In professional settings, clarity of intentions can enhance leadership and teamwork as it sets a clear direction and inspires others to contribute towards shared objectives. Setting clear intentions is more than meets the eye. By doing so, it will help you navigate conflicts and misunderstandings more effectively.

When you articulate your true motivations, you have the opportunity to address concerns, find common ground with others, and have more attuned interactions. So what are your intentions? Taking time to reflect on this question sets you on the path to becoming empowered and a greater opportunity to get your needs met.

EXERCISE: EXPLORING YOUR WANTS, NEEDS, EXPECTATIONS, AND INTENTIONS

This exercise encourages self-awareness and intentional living, helping you to align your actions with your true desires, needs, and deeper intentions.

Part 1: Exploring Your Wants

- **Find a Quiet Space:** Ensure you're in a comfortable, quiet environment where you can focus without interruptions.
- **Reflect:** Close your eyes and think about what excites and motivates you. Consider your passions, dreams, and what brings you joy.
- **Write Down Your Wants:** In a notebook, jot down what comes to mind. Use these prompts:
  o What do I want in my personal relationships with others?
  o What do I want in my relationship with myself?
  o What do I want in my career?
  o What hobbies or activities do I want to pursue?
  o What are my intentions behind these wants? (For example, the intention to grow, to connect deeply, to learn, etc.)
- **Prioritize:** Highlight the top three to five most important wants and their corresponding intentions.

Part 2: Identifying Your Needs

- **Reflect on Basic Needs**: Think about what you need for well-being—consider physical, emotional, social, and financial needs.
- **Write Down Your Needs and Intentions**: List your needs using these prompts:
  o What do I need to feel safe and secure?
  o What do I need for my physical health?
  o What emotional support do I need?
  o What are my intentions behind meeting these needs? (For example, the intention to feel safe, to be healthy, to be emotionally balanced, etc.)
- **Evaluate**: Reflect on whether these needs are currently being met and what steps you can take if they're not.

Part 3: Understanding Your Expectations and Intentions

- Reflect on Your Expectations of Yourself: Reflect on what you expect from yourself in different areas of your life. Consider both your strengths and areas where you want to grow.
  o What standards do I hold myself to in my work and personal life?

- o What do I expect from myself in terms of self-care and personal development?
- o What are my intentions behind these expectations? (For example, the intention to excel, to grow, to nurture myself, etc.)
- **Think about Your Expectations of Others:** Think about your relationships and what you expect from the people around you. Consider family, friends, colleagues, and partners.
  - o What do I expect from others in terms of support, communication, and respect?
  - o How do I communicate these expectations?
  - o What are my intentions behind these expectations? (For example, the intention to build trust, to have clear communication, to feel respected, etc.)
- **Write Down Your Expectations and Intentions:** Create two lists in your notebook—one for your expectations of yourself and one for your expectations of others. Be specific and realistic.
- **Reflect and Adjust:** Review your lists and consider if your expectations are fair and achievable. Think about any adjustments you might need to make to ensure they are reasonable and compassionate.

Part 4: Creating an Action Plan

- **Set Goals**: Based on your reflections, set specific goals to align your wants, needs, and expectations. Write down actionable steps.
- **Create a Timeline**
  o Establish a realistic timeline for each goal.
  o Journal your thoughts.
  o Write down any insights or thoughts from this exercise.

Exploring your wants, needs, expectations, and intentions creates the opportunity for you to gain a deeper understanding of yourself and create a more fulfilling and balanced life.

SECTION 3:
GET UNSTUCK BY
REINVENTING YOUR STORY

CHAPTER 5: THE STORIES WE TELL

"Our stories are also about self-protection...
But this unconscious storytelling leaves us
stuck."

—Brené Brown

My grandmother was always telling us a story about something. While telling the stories she would often crack herself up laughing as she sat fanning herself in her favorite chair.

My brother and I would be dropped off at my grandmother's house after school where we would wait for our parents to come home from work. We would trudge up the steps, backpacks slung over our shoulders, and knock on the glass sliding door. Oh, the smells! The wonderful smells of something home-made cooking would waft through the air like a dancing cloud. All we wanted to do was drop off those book bags and go back outside to play, which she allowed most times. Going back outside would come with a story and very specific instructions on what we could and could not do.

My grandmother had the most incredible way of telling us stories about people she had known through the years and conversations she found to be absolutely hilarious. Half the time, we had no idea what her stories were about. They were full of references to unfamiliar people and events. But it didn't matter. There was always a lesson woven into her tales, nuggets of wisdom that would only make sense years later. She would also tell us about all kinds of situations she had experienced or witnessed as a way of cautioning us to stay away from trouble. Her laughter was so infectious and would fill the room with warmth, and she would have a two-liter bottle of Mountain Dew sitting near.

"Go on outside," she would say, "but stay where I can see you." Huh? Stay where you can see us? That meant we had to stay on the porch because she wasn't going outside. She would look through the glass door to watch us. Why would she do this to us? That was not what we wanted to hear and certainly not going to work for us. All the action was taking place on the side of the building. This just didn't make sense. Why couldn't we go where our friends were? They were on the side of the building, not on the porch!

Well, her worries came from somewhere. She told the story about a little child playing outside who had gone out of the sight of the caring adults. Serious harm came to the child, and she did not want that for us. Being the invincible children that we were (wink wink), this made no sense to us.

Did we test the waters and venture around the corner? Of course. Did she know when we thought she didn't know? Yes, as I would hear my name echoing between the buildings, and we would come running back. She made it unequivocally clear there are consequences to not listening and following her directions. What came next?

The ultimate lesson: we had to come inside and hear another story. A story of some person, somewhere that something happened to, and then we would hear things like "you gon' learn" and "you don't believe fat meat is greasy."

It is only now that I can understand and appreciate the true value of my grandmother's stories. Ultimately, she was conveying to us the great responsibility she had to watch us and keep us safe. Returning us home to our parents all in one piece was her great responsibility.

Those stories were not just about the people or events themselves but about the virtues and lessons they embodied. Listening, following directions, staying safe—these were the real subjects of her tales. Each story was like a thread in a rich tapestry, weaving together the values and wisdom of generations past.

THE TRAVELING GENERATIONAL STORIES

Our parents also carried with them the stories and experiences of their parents, who had received them from their parents before them. It's like a vast, intricate web of knowledge and wisdom, and many times fears and hardships also, passed down from one generation to the next. Whether we realize it or not, we are all beneficiaries of this legacy.

The stories we hear and the lessons we learn shape us in ways we might not immediately recognize. But there's an interesting twist to this generational storytelling. Each person who repeats a story adds their own interpretation, their own spin. It's like a giant game of telephone. The core message sometimes remains, but it goes through our different filters, and on top of that the story will be skewed and colored by the listener's own experiences and perspectives.

My grandmother's stories, for instance, were shaped by her life in a small, rural town, her experiences during the Civil Rights era, her enduring faith, as well as any trauma that she may have experienced but did not share with us. When she told us these stories, they were infused with her unique experiences and intended to guide us and set us on a path not like her own.

When I retell my grandmother's stories, I add my own layer of interpretation. I might emphasize different aspects or draw different lessons based on what stood out to me along with my own life experiences. Although the essence of the stories tends to remain, they grow and change with each retelling, becoming richer and more nuanced and sometimes heavier.

It's a reminder of the profound impact of storytelling. Stories are powerful tools for expression, teaching, preserving history and culture, and for connecting us across generations. They remind us of where we come from, and they help guide us as we move forward.

Whenever I think back to those afternoons at my grandmother's house, I'm filled with greater understanding. Her stories were more than just her telling us about some random people. Instead, she was sharing wisdom about life that we had yet to live. Each story, each lesson, is a link in the chain that connects us to our past. Storytelling is powerful and can shape the way in which we see and understand ourselves within the world.

TRAUMA SHATTERS OUR STORIES

When a traumatic event occurs, it takes a profound toll on the survivor's ability to recall and retell stories, both recent and generational ones, which forever changes their narratives from that moment forward.

That traumatic experience can happen early in childhood or in adulthood. When you experience trauma, the flow of your life story is disrupted. Instead of a coherent and seamless narrative, you are most likely left with disjointed pieces of stories that are difficult to place together. At whatever point in life trauma occurs, what is left behind are fragmented stories and a profound sense of disconnection to the world around us.

When a person is attempting to recount the traumatic experience, it can feel like trying to piece together a five-thousand-piece puzzle or the fragments and shards of a shattered mirror. Trying to put the story back together in a coherent way is profoundly difficult. This disconnection between the experience and the ability to articulate it can be deeply isolating, leaving you feeling misunderstood and alone in your pain.

The disconnection is rooted in the brain's response to trauma. During a traumatic event, the brain's alarm system (the amygdala) goes into overdrive, flooding the body with stress hormones, adrenaline and cortisol. It becomes hyperactive, while the hippocampus (our memory storage system which helps form and organize memories) becomes impaired. As a result, memories of the traumatic event can become fragmented, disjointed, and difficult to recall in any kind of linear fashion. The flow of these hormones coupled with the alarm system going off, interferes with the brain's ability to process and store memories accurately. The heightened state of arousal makes it difficult to process the trauma logically and can lead to intrusive memories and flashbacks, which only further complicates your ability to narrate the experience coherently.

This biological response that our brain and body experiences is a protective mechanism. If you ask me, the brain is a magical organ that simply blows me away when I consider all that it is capable of doing! But while the brain and body are working hard to protect us in this way, it can leave us struggling to make sense of some of our experiences.

If you've had a traumatic experience, you might find it difficult to recount the details and may struggle with reconnecting with yourself and loved ones. Let me tell you, this is normal. You are having a normal response to an abnormal experience. Your brain's job is to protect you at all costs in the way it is designed to do. It does this by dissociating you from the experience, which is a coping mechanism where the person detaches from the reality of what happened.

While this will oftentimes provide a temporary relief, it also interferes with the ability to process and integrate the trauma story into the rest of your life story. If you are unable to fully articulate and understand what happened, the trauma remains an open wound. It will continuously affect your mental and emotional health and exacerbate the sense of isolation.

ARE YOU CARRYING TOO MANY BAGS?

These burdens sit atop the already heavy load of inherited and societal pressures that many individuals, particularly women and women of color, carry. Legacy burdens, such as familial expectations and cultural stereotypes, only compound the weight of the personal trauma experienced. This layered burden can make the path to healing seem daunting, as it involves untangling not just the recent trauma but also the deep-seated, intergenerational wounds.

The burdens left behind by trauma are not only immediate but also long lasting. On an emotional level, there is the pain of the experience itself, compounded by feelings of shame, guilt, and helplessness, which can lead to a sense of unresolved tension within the body and ongoing distress. The intensity of the emotions can be overwhelming and pervasive, affecting every aspect of your life. It interferes with your social game, leading to isolation and withdrawal from others to avoid triggering memories or because you think no one understands what you are going through, and you can't explain it. This cycle of disconnection from your support systems only exacerbates the sense of isolation and can get in the way of the healing process.

When the burden of the trauma lands on top of the burdens passed down through generations, the weight can become unbearable. Now adding the pain of personal trauma creates a compounded effect, where you are now navigating both your inherited struggles and your own direct traumatic experiences. Pure weight. This is the unexplainable heaviness. It's like carrying on your shoulder your grandmother's designer purse, mom's designer purse, and your designer purse. Now you know grandma's purse is ridiculously heavy and mom's purse makes absolutely no sense. What is in those things? This triple load can lead to a sense of despair, like the weight of the world is on your shoulders. It can't keep going.

KNOWLEDGE IS THE FIRST STEP TOWARD HEALING

Healing from trauma involves gradually piecing together the shattered fragments of one's story and finding a way to integrate them into a cohesive narrative. That narrative may happen verbally or nonverbally. This process is not easy and often requires professional support, such as therapy, to navigate. It also involves acknowledging and addressing both the immediate burdens of the trauma and the legacy burdens that have compounded the experience.

Recognizing that these are the challenges you are facing and understanding the brain's response to trauma is the first step toward healing. When you can acknowledge the need for therapeutic support to help through the layers of burdens, then you can begin to reconstruct your shattered story and begin to integrate your experiences to find a sense of self, continuity, and peace. By doing so, you can begin to deconstruct a disjointed narrative and rewrite your story with new understanding to heal the deep wounds left by trauma. You will reconnect with yourself and others and rebuild a sense of wholeness to your story and to your life.

Every day, remind yourself of these powerful truths:

"I have the power to choose my thoughts, feelings, and actions."

"I have the strength to move beyond the past and create a brighter future."

"I have the ability to rewrite my story."

EXERCISE: WHAT STORY ARE YOU TELLING?

This exercise aims to help you identify the story you are currently telling yourself about your life; recognize any negative or limiting narratives; and imagine a different, more empowering story. This process can aid in understanding how your self-perception influences your actions and well-being and can help you reframe your narrative to support your personal growth and healing.

1. **Find a quiet and comfortable place** where you can reflect without interruptions. Take a few deep breaths to center yourself and clear your mind.

2. **Current Story Reflection**
   o Begin by writing down the story you are currently telling yourself about your life.

This can include your thoughts about your past, your present situation, and your future.

- o Consider aspects such as your relationships, career, personal achievements, challenges, and your sense of self-worth. Be as honest and detailed as possible.
- o Reflect on any recurring themes or patterns in your story. Do you notice any negative or limiting beliefs? For example, do you often think, "I am not good enough," "I always fail," or "I can't trust anyone"?

3. **Identify the Impact**
   - o Write down how this current story makes you feel. Does it bring you a sense of empowerment, or does it weigh you down?
   - o Consider how this story affects your actions and decisions. Does it motivate you to pursue your goals, or does it hold you back?
   - o Reflect on the origins of this story. Are there specific events, experiences, or influences (such as family, society, or culture) that have shaped this narrative?

CHAPTER 6: BREAKING DOWN THE STORY

"Our thoughts affect our agreement with reality, our story we tell ourselves. If you want to change your story, start with your thoughts."

—Tony Curl

In the journey of personal growth and healing, one critical step is restructuring the stories we tell ourselves. These narratives are often deeply ingrained and rooted in our past experiences and shape our beliefs, perceptions, and behaviors. Restructuring the way we see and understand experiences is a crucial technique that allows us to dismantle our old stories and false beliefs that contribute to carrying unnecessary burdens. By providing evidence to counter negative self-perceptions and self-talk, you can begin to recreate what you want your story to be.

THE MESSAGE

From the moment we are born, we are receiving messages. These messages tend to differ for cisgender boys and girls, and certainly for transgender and non-binary individuals. Society sends these macro messages of how we are to understand our roles and how we are to behave in the world, what we can or cannot have, or where we should live or not live. Believe it or not society even tells us how we should think, what we can and cannot read, and what women can and cannot do with their own bodies.

There is so much more that society sends to us that ultimately shapes our individual worlds. We should also be aware of the messages passed down from generation to generation. These messages tend to shape us and create an understanding of ourselves on a more micro level. As we matriculate through life these messages become our roadmap for how to interpret and navigate our experiences.

Cognitive restructuring involves identifying and challenging negative thought patterns and replacing them with more accurate and helpful perspectives. This process requires you to examine the evidence supporting your beliefs and consider alternative interpretations. By reframing your thoughts, you can shift your mindset from one of self-doubt and criticism to one of self-compassion and empowerment.

THE EXAMINATION

Distorted stories woven intricately over time can shape your perceptions and guide your actions. When those distorted stories are replayed on repetitive loops of thought, they confine you to a singular perspective of yourself. It's so easy to fall into believing that these stories define you, that they represent the unchangeable essence of who you are. "This is my life," you may be saying to yourself, further exacerbating that feeling of being resigned to the familiar script you have carried for years.

But the beautiful truth is that the stories you have been telling yourself are *not* unchangeable truths. They are narratives based on the interpretation of experiences lived by you and by many others, and as the creator of your own stories you hold the power to untangle and deconstruct the stories and then rewrite them.

You are the author, the storyteller of your life, capable of infusing your narratives with new meaning, purpose, and direction. Just imagine yourself reclaiming your narrative, stepping into a space where you have control over the plot twists and development of characters. The process of reconstruction consists of confronting the loops of thought that have held you captive. And when you do, you'll discover that what once seemed like an unchangeable script turns out to be an adaptable narrative, ripe with opportunities for revision and renewal.

Of course, there will be challenges. Peeling back the layers of your inner narrative can be like standing naked in front of a mirror. While some may like what they see, for many this can be very scary. You may find yourself working really hard to avoid it like the plague. It will require courage for you to challenge the familiar, embrace uncertainty, and face new possibilities.

Yet dissecting our internal dialogue, examining its origins, and questioning its validity is only the beginning to creating new understanding. The braver you become by being vulnerable, the better you will be able to rewrite the narratives from a place of empowerment.

WHAT YOU STAND TO GAIN

Breaking down those old stories is extremely important for your growth and emotional health. It starts with spotting and facing those limiting beliefs that have been stuck in your mind for ages. When you start to identify those limiting beliefs, we start to see where our fears, insecurities, and self-imposed limits come from, which leads to a big sense of emotional freedom.

This journey helps us understand what triggers our emotions and behaviors, so we can handle life's challenges more thoughtfully and genuinely. These beliefs often hold us back from reaching our full potential and seizing new opportunities, but when these narratives are broken down, you will start to understand what triggers your thoughts and behaviors. Having this understanding can set you free emotionally and help you gain skills to *respond* to situations more thoughtfully rather than simply *reacting* to them.

The presence of old narratives often will keep you stuck in a fixed view of yourself. Learning to break them down, creates opportunities for you to open up to new possibilities and potentials that exist within. It becomes necessary to explore alternative perspectives and opportunities that may have been overshadowed by old, rigid ways of thinking.

This shift in mindset creates a sense of resilience and adaptability that will move you to navigate life with greater flexibility. It also aligns you more closely with your authentic self, helping you discern between societal expectations and what are to be your true values and aspirations. With the ability to tell yourself a new narrative, you now can begin to see different paths and outcomes for your life, which further helps to develop a mindset of growth and resilience.

Relationally, deconstructing internal narratives can significantly improve your interactions with others. It enables you to challenge prejudgments and biases that may color your perceptions of people and situations. By letting go of negative or judgmental narratives, you cultivate empathy, compassion, and deeper connections based on genuine clear understanding. This transformation not only enriches your relationships but also contributes to a more supportive social environment.

This process of deconstructing old narratives contributes to your overall mental and emotional well-being. It reduces the stress and anxiety that often accompany rigid thinking patterns and negative self-talk. As you release outdated beliefs and embrace more empowering narratives, you create space for inner peace, self-acceptance, and self-compassion.

The journey to self-empowerment and self-responsibility is by deconstructing these old internal narratives. It allows you to reclaim ownership of your thoughts, emotions, and choices, moving away from passive acceptance of circumstances and more towards active engagement in shaping your reality. This creates the freedom and internal security for you to rewrite your life story in ways that reflect your authentic self in the present and empower you to live more purposefully and joyfully.

I hope that you can see that there is a common theme here. The old stories that are on repeat are dated and certainly keep you somewhere in the past. They interfere with you having the best opportunity to live in the present. In essence, breaking down old internal narratives is like a superfood, rich in nutrients for your soul. It creates a process that will boost your self-awareness, emotional intelligence, and personal empowerment.

It is time to let go of the belief that the story you've carried all these years must define your future. Give yourself the chance to embrace the truth that you are both the advocate and the narrator. Your story does not have to be predetermined; instead, it is an ongoing creation, shaped by your lived experiences, choices, beliefs, and aspirations for your future. You have permission to step into the role of the storyteller, weaving a narrative that resonates with your deepest desires, truths, and aspirations.

EXERCISE: IMAGINING A DIFFERENT STORY

This exercise aims to transform your current narrative into a more positive and empowering story about your life. By identifying and changing negative or limiting beliefs, you can envision a new path forward that inspires hope, motivation, and a sense of possibility.

1. **Find a quiet and comfortable place** where you can reflect without distractions. Take several deep breaths to help center yourself and clear your mind.

2. **Reflect and Imagine**
   o Find a quiet space where you can relax and focus without distractions. Close your eyes and take a few deep breaths to center yourself.
   o Visualize your life without the negative or limiting aspects of your current story. Imagine overcoming challenges, achieving your goals, and feeling confident and worthy.

o With your journal and pen ready, write down this new story for yourself. Include positive affirmations, aspirations, and details of how you envision your life.

3. **Explore Your Feelings**:

o As you write your new story, pay attention to how it makes you feel. Does it inspire hope, motivation, and a sense of possibility?

o Reflect on how you would act differently in this new narrative. Consider the behaviors, attitudes, and choices that align with this empowering story.

4. **Bridge the Gap**

o After envisioning your new story, reflect on the changes needed to transition from your current narrative to this imagined one.

o Write down small, actionable steps you can take to start shifting your narrative. These steps could include:

■ Practicing positive affirmations daily.

■ Setting achievable goals that align with your new story.

■ Seeking support from friends, family, or a mentor who believes in your potential.

- Engaging in self-care activities that promote well-being and positivity.

5. **Commit to Change**
   o Commit to regularly revisiting and refining your new story. Use your journal to track your progress, celebrate successes, and adjust your approach as needed.
   o Stay mindful of any negative thoughts or beliefs that may try to creep back in. Challenge them with the positive aspects of your new narrative.

6. **Embrace Growth and Transformation**
   o Embrace this exercise as an ongoing practice of growth and transformation. Your new story is a reflection of your evolving beliefs, aspirations, and actions.
   o Trust in your ability to create a life that aligns with your true potential and inspires you to thrive.

By engaging in this exercise regularly, you can cultivate a mindset that supports your journey toward a more fulfilling and empowering life story.

CHAPTER 7: REWRITING
THE STORY

"When we deny the story, it defines us. When we own the story, we can write a brave new ending."

— **Brene Brown**

One Sunday afternoon I found myself going back and forth with myself. It was that ole nagging voice that lingers around saying "you should be cleaning up and washing clothes and preparing to cook dinner." I realized, however, it had been an extremely busy week and my whole Saturday was full with dance class, taking care of my mother, grocery shopping, and being my children's personal Uber. I was tired.

I began to counter the nag with just those facts. I had not had any opportunity to just be still. By panning out and taking stock of the prior the weeks, I realized I needed to give myself some compassion and grace, considering my busy schedule over the last few weeks.

So, I changed the internal dialogue and decided to give myself permission to take a break. I wanted to just get lost in watching television and slow my thinking down and float off into never-never land. After spending a lot of time surfing the channels, I decided I wanted to laugh a little. I landed on the Netflix special *Kevin Hart: Mark Twain Prize for American Humor*. Some of my favorite comedians were honoring him and as the show went along, I noticed a common theme that was present when they each gave their presentation. They all spoke to his being a dreamer. I could relate to that. I am a dreamer too.

He had a desire to succeed and would ask the greats what he needed to do to get where they were. He was a student of the craft and took the feedback from the greats seriously, which lead him to sell out arenas and stadiums unlike any before him. While I haven't sold out arenas *yet* (my dreamer self says), I too have been a student of my craft and have asked the greats of my field questions and asked for mentorship.

YOUR INTERNAL MESSAGING

While the show was funny, I was inspired. It resonated with me. It reminded me that it is not too late for me to strive for my dreams. That there is a pathway forward; I just need to seek it out and ask the best people the best questions. You never know where your inspiration will come from, but allowing yourself to be open to possibility can lead you to places you never thought were possible.

I gained more from watching that show than I could have imagined. I can still rewrite my story to include my dream. I could hear that voice speaking, that old narrative of dreams are just dreams, and you need to lean into what will put food on the table. I actually recognized that this narrative wasn't mine, but it was passed down to me. The idea that the dream may not be lucrative enough to be self-sustaining. Go for something that is more of a guarantee to put food on your table and a roof over your head.

Instead, I told myself I can pursue my dreams and create a narrative that is fitting for here and now not the past and not for others who have passed down their baggage to me. My dream is not deferred. So, that old narrative that "dreams are just that, dreams" doesn't have to be true for me. I can counter the old internal dialogue to make room for rewriting my story. The power is within me to bring this dream to life.

There were a few things that took place here in this story that can change the way you tell your own story. In stepping back and giving myself permission to rest, I began to change the tone of my internal dialogue. Recognizing the need for compassion for myself and then developing the goals that would lead me to the desired dream outcome. So how can you stop the loop of the negative internal dialogue that tells that old story and keeps us stuck?

Here are three ideas:

CHECK YOUR TONE: IT MATTERS

Who are you talking to like that? I find myself asking my children that question when they respond to me with a bit of sass, wait, no, actually a bunch of sass. "You can have a point, but you will need to be respectful when talking to me," I say. Of course, this is much different from when I was growing up, when you didn't dare say a thing, let alone try and make a point. I wanted to do it differently, to rewrite the narrative, and make the experience for my children a little better; however, I wouldn't dare let them talk to me in just any kind of way.

So, why would I allow myself to say all kinds of mean things and in the nastiest tone to myself.

There is no good reason to talk to yourself in just any kind of way.

How you relate to you is the blueprint for how you let others treat you. Let's think about this for a moment. If I talk to myself in an aggressive manner, when someone else is talking to me in the same manner, I may not recognize it. This comes from somewhere, and the polyvagal theory developed by Dr. Stephen Porges can help to make sense of it all. Let me explain.

There are three main principles to the polyvagal theory: autonomic nervous system (ANS), neuroception, and co-regulation. The ANS is separated into three parts: (1) the dorsal vagal, which brings about immobilization; (2) the ventral vagal, which allows for the ability to feel safe and connected; and (3) the sympathetic system, which controls the fight or flight mode. The focus is on the role of the vagus nerve in regulating our emotional responses and social behaviors (Dana, 2020).

Neuroception is the second principle, and it is how our nervous system automatically senses safety or danger without us even realizing it. Unlike the concept of perception, which is a more conscious process, neuroception works in the background and triggers changes in our body based on what feels safe or threatening, even when we know something is not posing a danger. It is constantly listening for what is safe and what is not (Dana, 2020). If you are only familiar with harsh tones of voice, then your ability to decipher danger may be skewed. Your tone of voice matters.

The third principle, co-regulation, is that our ANS learns to self-regulate as we grow from a baby to adulthood. The ANS gradually learns to calm itself down from stress as you grow older. In order to do this, it starts with the ability to co-regulate or mirroring the calm or stress of others, such as a child being soothed by a parent or caregiver. Even as we develop self-regulation, co-regulation remains to be valuable in various situations like therapy (Dana, 2020).

Oftentimes people are not aware of the way in which they talk to themselves internally. It just is; that is how it has always been. One possible explanation could be that a person has learned this from hearing other people speak to them in such a tone. Or it could be they don't feel good about themselves, and their internal dialogue reflects that. To notice how you are speaking to yourself is a step toward adjusting your relationship to yourself.

When we feel safe and in the ventral vagal state, our "social engagement system" is activated. This allows us to connect with others, feel calm, and be open. This state often develops from having caregivers treat us kindly, listen to us, and make us feel secure. This is called attunement—when our caregivers are in tune with our needs and emotions, making us feel understood and safe.

If our caregivers often make us feel unsafe through harsh words or neglect, however, our nervous system adapts by becoming more sensitive to threats. This is called misattunement—when there's a disconnect between our needs and how they are met. We might start talking to ourselves in the same harsh way, mirroring how we were treated.

Over time, this becomes our blueprint. We might not recognize aggressive or unsafe behavior from others because it feels normal to us. Our nervous system is used to it. So, if you talk to yourself in a safe and compassionate way, you are more likely to recognize and reject unsafe treatment from others. Conversely, if you are harsh with yourself, you may unconsciously accept similar behavior from others, perpetuating a cycle of misattunement.

BE GOOD TO YOURSELF

What does your internal dialogue sound like?

Being around a person who is nagging, critical, impatient, or just simply rude is miserable and something we typically try to avoid. Why, then, are we nagging, critical, impatient, and rude to ourselves?

I challenge you to speak to yourself the way you would speak to a person who means the world to you. Be encouraging and supportive, which is different from nagging. You can offer constructive criticism, which is different from being critical. You can gently encourage movement and yet still be patient. It is these qualities that build empathy and allow you to show compassion toward yourself.

I encourage you to work toward cultivating a more positive and compassionate inner dialogue, which is a cornerstone of cognitive restructuring. When you challenge and reframe your limiting beliefs, you can break free from the constraints of your past and embrace a more hopeful and optimistic outlook on your life. This process requires courage and vulnerability to confront deeply ingrained beliefs and challenge the stories you have told yourself for years.

As you embark on this journey of self-discovery and growth, it's essential to ask yourself Do I have compassion for myself? If not, do I *want* to have compassion for myself?

Growing in self-compassion and self-acceptance is crucial in the process of shedding burdens and rewriting your story. Unlike harsh self-criticism and judgment, self-compassion requires you to treat yourself with kindness, understanding, and acceptance, especially in moments of struggle and difficulty.

Throughout this journey toward greater self-understanding, it is essential to recognize that change takes time, so you need to have patience with yourself. Shedding old stories and rewriting your narrative is not a linear process but rather a journey of zig zags and steps taken forward and backward. Along the way, although you may encounter setbacks and challenges, these moments provide opportunities for you to learn more about you and your growth work.

The goal of restructuring the way you think and practicing self-compassion is all about giving yourself the freedom to live authentically and bravely. It's shedding the old layers of past beliefs and self-imposed limitations that have been holding you back and weighing you down. Think of it as a chance to rewrite your inner script. By questioning and challenging the old stories you've told yourself and replacing them with a kinder, more supportive inner dialogue, you're setting yourself up for a life that's more aligned with who you really are and who you want to be. It's about moving away from self-criticism and embracing self-acceptance. Self-acceptance is the golden ticket to opening the doors to new opportunities and a life beyond what you could ever imagine.

REMEMBER YOUR MAP

When you take the time to reflect on what you truly want, need, and expect from yourself, you're essentially drawing a map for your new story. It's like figuring out the roadmap for a journey that's uniquely yours. This reflection helps you get clear on your core values, passions, and goals, making it easier to align your actions with your true self. As you become more in tune with your authentic desires and aspirations, you'll find it easier to set meaningful goals and make choices that resonate with who you are at your core.

Ultimately, healing from trauma is a multifaceted process that requires patience, compassion, and a willingness to explore both your mind and body. By leveraging the insights from polyvagal theory and engaging in practices that promote regulation and connection, you can begin to unpack those designer bags of trauma. This journey is not easy, but it is possible, and it leads to a future where you are no longer held captive by your past but rather empowered by your resilience and newly created capacity for healing.

EXERCISE: IDENTIFYING SELF-TALK & REWRITING YOUR INNER NARRATIVE

This exercise is designed to help you become more aware of your inner dialogue, identify negative self-talk patterns, and empower you to rewrite your narrative with kindness and self-compassion.

1. **Find a quiet and comfortable place** where you can reflect without distractions. Take several deep breaths to help center yourself and clear your mind.

2. **Reflect on some** internal dialogue you had during a moment of exhaustion.
   - Questions to Consider:
     - What did your inner voice say to you?
     - Was it critical, supportive, or indifferent?
     - How did this internal dialogue affect your feelings and actions?
   - Transcribe the thoughts you had, noting any patterns of negative self-talk or self-compassion.

3. **Analyze Your Inner Voice:** Compare the critical and supportive voices you identified. Recognize the sources of your negative self-talk.

   o Where do these critical thoughts come from? Are they echoes of past experiences or external influences?

   o Consider how your inner dialogue might be influenced by your sense of safety and past experiences, as explained by polyvagal theory.

4. **Reframe Your Thoughts:** Practice cognitive restructuring by challenging and reframing your limiting beliefs.

   o For each negative thought, write a compassionate and supportive counter-thought.

   o For example: "I should be more productive" can be countered with "It's okay to rest when I'm tired. I deserve a break."

5. **Visualize Self-Compassion**

   • Close your eyes and imagine a scenario where you treat yourself with the same kindness and compassion you would offer a loved one. How does this compassionate version of yourself speak and act? What emotions arise when you visualize this kindness?

- Develop a short, affirming statement that you can repeat to yourself during moments of stress or exhaustion. For example:
  - "I am worthy of rest and relaxation."
  - "I am doing my best, and that is enough."

By practicing self-compassion and rewriting your inner narrative, you can shift from self-criticism to self-empowerment, fostering greater resilience and kindness toward yourself.

SECTION 4:
GET UNSTUCK BY
CREATING HEALING
CONNECTIONS

CHAPTER 8: CONNECT
TO THE SELF

"To know yourself is the beginning of all
wisdom."

– Aristotle

What if I told you that there may be several different parts of you that exist today? That were born with these parts of you, but the role that these parts have taken on were due to the experiences you had in your lifetime. It's nothing like the movie *Sybil* type thing, where you have multiple personalities, as they used to say, but rather we have an internal system that governs our way of being.

One of the key frameworks for understanding these different parts is the Internal Family Systems (IFS) developed by Dr. Richard Schwartz, a leading researcher and trauma therapist. According to IFS, our internal system consists of three different parts— manager, firefighter, and exile—each with its own role and function. The framework provides a way to understand our internal dialogue and how these parts interact with each other and influence our behavior and emotions. It offers a way to understand how we can view our inner world and begin to create internal peace.

The primary role of the *manager* parts is to maintain control and order in your life. The manager parts of you are proactive and often takes on responsibilities to prevent problems before they arise. This part of you is concerned with keeping you safe, managing your daily activities, and ensuring you meet your goals. These parts work to create stability and predictability and often have a strong influence on how you approach challenges and maintain your routines. Your manager parts can be critical and perfectionistic, striving to ensure that everything is in its proper place.

The *firefighter* parts, on the other hand, comes into play when there is a crisis or emotional upheaval. Their role is to quickly address and extinguish any emotional fires that may arise. The firefighters are reactive and can engage in behaviors that provide immediate relief or distraction, such as substance use or emotional eating. The firefighter parts work to alleviate the intense discomfort or distress that might otherwise overwhelm you. While their actions can be disruptive, they intend to protect you from feeling too much pain or discomfort.

Lastly, the *exile* parts of you hold painful memories, emotions, or experiences that have been suppressed or rejected. The exile parts are often associated with past traumas or deep-seated fears and are typically kept hidden from your conscious awareness.

The exile parts are vulnerable and sensitive, and their experiences are often the root cause of emotional struggles. By understanding and addressing these exile parts, you can work toward healing and integrating your past experiences into your overall sense of self. Recognizing the roles and functions of these different parts helps you gain insight into your internal dynamics and fosters personal growth and self-compassion.

SHE'S EXPECTING YOU

In the Internal Family Systems, Self energy refers to the core of who you are—your authentic, compassionate, and grounded self. When you are operating from Self energy, you are present, calm, and able to navigate your inner system with clarity and empathy. This part of you acts as a compassionate leader, capable of understanding and integrating the different parts of your internal system.

You have the capacity to listen to your manager parts, soothe your firefighter parts, and address the needs of your exile parts with compassion, curiosity, clarity, calmness, connection, confidence, creativity, and courage. When you are centered in Self energy, you can engage with your internal world in a way that leans into healing and peace, allowing you to respond to life's challenges with resilience and grace.

She's been expecting you for some time now. Your Self has always been there; you just had to meet her. All of your parts have worked overtime and very hard to protect you and keep you afloat. You made it. While it may have felt as though your body failed you, in actuality it worked overtime. You now understand that your brain and your body are connected, and it did the best it could at the time to protect you. You are now connected to you.

It may take some time to become fully comfortable with you and to fully trust and grow into you. We want to extend gratitude to all of the parts that worked overtime to keep you safe and get you this far. It is hard out here in these streets to just sit with yourself. Quietness can be the enemy. There will be a day when sitting with yourself will no longer feel daunting and scary, but will give you peace and comfort. You are on that path to a deeper understanding and acceptance of yourself.

REWRITING SELF-CARE

We always talk about self-care. You need to make sure that you are doing self-care, they say. I even used the phrase earlier in this book. Well, let's look at this more deeply. Is it a massage you say to yourself? Is it going out buying yourself a bunch of stuff? Or is it getting a manicure and pedicure, or even warm bubble bath? I say, not so much. Self-care is not a massage or getting your nails done per se. These things are all temporary and have a short life. I see you with your head turned to the side thinking, *Wait, what?*

Stay with me here. I'm going somewhere with all of this.

On a recent vacation, I had been looking forward to getting a massage and facial. I was so excited to just rest my mind and relax my muscles because it had been a long few months. The facial was a bonus, cause why not nurture my facial skin as well?

As my massage and facial got underway, my thoughts started running like they were in the Olympic trials. I spent the first forty minutes of a seventy-minute massage and facial trying to stop those racing thoughts and to relax and just be present in the moment. You'd think I would know how to do this as I tell my clients to do this for a living. But it's not easy for any of us to take fifty to ninety minutes and just have quiet thoughts. It's an art. It's something we have to practice.

And we should practice. Relaxing our bodies and our minds is a good thing.

But is this the epitome of self-care? Some people might think so. And I believe it certainly is a layer of self-care. But let's go a little deeper, shall we? Let's take a look at those Olympic trial thoughts. Why were they racing in the first place? Could it be that as soon as I got still for a moment, my brain freaked-out and didn't want me to forget all the things I thought I should be doing at the moment? All the expectations I thought I should have been meeting, regardless of whether they were realistic or not? Remnants of shattered narratives I may still have needed to deconstruct and rewrite?

I want to go there for a moment. What if *healing* is self-care? What if the *process* of healing is self-care? What if gaining the knowledge that understanding your past leads you to your present and future is self-care? What if making a better brain-body connection is self-care? What if knowing that your body holds the key to your healing is self-care? What if having the ability to identify and abandon burdens that are not actually ours to carry is self-care?

All that to say, what if self-care is more than temporary good feelings? What if it's the hard task of working through past experiences and making peace with your past? Or crying and expressing painful thoughts to get them outside of yourself? Or facing the scariest parts of your past or rewriting the stories you tell yourself? Or reaching the point where you no longer avoid the pain and defer your dreams but connect with yourself in a way that you never thought possible?

EXERCISE: CONNECTING WITH YOURSELF AND EXPLORING YOUR DIFFERENT PARTS

This exercise is designed to help you connect with and explore the different parts of yourself, fostering self-awareness, compassion, and balance. Each part of you has a purpose and a voice, and by honoring and integrating these parts, you create a stronger, more resilient self. You may need to give yourself multiple days to complete this exercise.

Step 1: Create a Comfortable Environment

1. **Find a Quiet Space**: Choose a peaceful, comfortable place where you won't be disturbed. You might want to light a candle, play soft music, or use a calming essential oil.

2. **Set Up**: Have a notebook or journal and a pen ready. Sit in a comfortable chair or lie down on a yoga mat.

Step 2: Grounding and Centering

1. **Deep Breathing**: Close your eyes and take a few deep breaths. Inhale through your nose, hold for a few seconds, and exhale through your mouth. Repeat until you feel calm and centered.

2. **Body Scan**: Starting at the top of your head, slowly scan down your body, noticing any areas of tension or discomfort. Consciously relax each part of your body as you go.

Step 3: Identify Different Parts of Yourself

1. Understand that each of us has different parts or aspects of our personality. These parts can include the inner child, the inner critic, the

nurturer, the achiever, and many more. Each part has its own voice and role in our lives.

2. **Visualization Exercise**:
   - *Close Your Eyes*: Imagine you are in a safe and comfortable room with several chairs. Each chair represents a different part of you.
   - *Invite Your Parts*: Visualize each part of yourself taking a seat in one of the chairs. As each part sits down, acknowledge its presence and purpose.
   - *Journal Prompt*: Write down the names of each part that comes to mind. Describe their characteristics, roles, and how they contribute to your life.

Step 4: Dialoguing with Your Parts

1. **Choose a Part**: Pick one part of yourself to focus on. This could be the part that is most vocal or the one you feel needs the most attention.

2. **Journal Dialogue**: Engage in a written conversation with this part of yourself.
   - Questions to Consider:
     - What is your purpose?
     - How do you try to help me?
     - What do you need from me?
   - Example Dialogue:

- You: "Hello, Inner Critic. What is your purpose in my life?"
- Inner Critic: "I try to protect you from failure by pointing out your mistakes."
- You: "Thank you for your intention. What do you need from me to feel more at ease?"

Step 5: Integrating and Balancing Your Parts

1. **Reflect on Needs**: Consider the needs of each part of yourself and how they might be met in a balanced way.
   - Journal Prompt: Write down the needs of each part and brainstorm ways to fulfill these needs. How can you nurture each part without letting any one part dominate?
   - Example: The achiever part might need goals and recognition, while the nurturer part might need rest and self-care.

2. **Affirmation Exercise**:
   - Create Affirmations: Develop affirmations that acknowledge and honor each part of yourself.
   - Example Affirmations:
     - "I appreciate my Inner Critic for wanting to keep me safe. I will listen with compassion."

- ▪ "I honor my Inner Child's need for play and joy. I will make time for fun."

Step 6: Visualization for Integration

1. **Guided Visualization**: Close your eyes and visualize a harmonious meeting between all parts of yourself.
   - o Imagine: See all your parts coming together in a circle, holding hands, and sharing their strengths and insights.
   - o Unifying Symbol: Picture a symbol or image that represents the unity and balance of all your parts. This could be a tree, a circle, or any symbol that feels right to you.
2. **Journal Reflection**: Write down your experience of the visualization. How did it feel to see all your parts working together? What symbol did you choose, and why?

Step 7: Ongoing Practice

1. **Daily Check-In**: Develop a daily practice of checking in with your different parts. Spend a few minutes each day journaling or meditating on how each part is feeling and what they need.
   - o Journal Prompt: How are my different parts feeling today? What do they need from me?

2. **Monthly Reflection**: Set a reminder to review your journal entries and reflect on your progress.

   o Journal Prompt: How have my different parts changed over the past month? What have I learned about myself?

CHAPTER 9: WHERE'S MY CREW?

"Healing takes place within the context of relationships, it cannot happen in isolation."

— **Dr. Bruce Perry**

"Alone we can do so little; together we can do so much."

— **Helen Keller**

The experience of a traumatic event can really shake up how you connect with people and the world around you. It often leaves you feeling isolated and hypervigilant, making it tough to have meaningful connections and relationships and feel like you belong.

Healing from trauma isn't just about getting through the pain; it's about connecting and feeling safe with others again.

When trauma disrupts your sense of safety, it can be difficult to trust again. Or if you have never trusted, it can be nearly impossible to trust at all. The heightened vigilance and fear that often follow traumatic experiences create barriers that tend to keep you from opening up to others.

So what does this look like? You may find yourself withdrawing from social interactions and avoiding opportunities to connect with those in your family, school, or workspace. You may feel like no one understands you and the experiences you are going through. This isolation can become a vicious cycle, making it even harder to heal and reconnect.

WHERE MY GIRLS AT?

Healing from trauma involves more than just addressing the emotional and psychological wounds; it's about rebuilding a foundation of trust, security, and connection. This process often requires creating new, positive experiences with others, ones that can counteract the negative impacts of trauma.

One of those ways is to find a therapist to build a safe and trusted connection. Working with someone who can help guide you to creating those new positive experiences. Another way is to find people who understand your journey and can offer empathy, support, and a sense of safety and validation.

You can find supportive people in various ways, such as joining a local support group for individuals with similar experiences, connecting with a trusted helping professional, participating in community programs, or engaging with a safe and encouraging online community, like a dedicated Facebook group. These supportive relationships play a significant role in helping you feel safe and connected again.

A supportive group of people who understand you can make all the difference. Your crew consists of those who accept you for who you are, where you are, and who offer a sense of belonging that the experience of trauma has taken away. Being part of a crew can help you feel seen and understood and less alone, while also providing a nurturing environment where you can begin to trust again.

Having a crew to help you rebuild trust, feel understood, and create the kind of connections helps you thrive. Surrounding yourself with people who genuinely care about your well-being and who can provide a safe space for you to express yourself is essential for your healing journey, as it allows you to share your experiences, receive support, and learn from others who have walked a similar path.

Reconnecting with others in a safe and nurturing environment is crucial for the healing journey, allowing you to restore the bonds that trauma once fractured. As you rebuild these connections, you'll find that you are not alone, and that your crew genuinely wants to be part of your healing process. Together, you can create a supportive network that encourages growth, resilience, and a renewed sense of belonging.

I attended an all-female concert where 98 percent of the attendees were women. It was a movement happening in the arena. I did not know anyone except for my good friend who is a part of my crew. Suddenly, I felt a synergy, a connectedness with the people in the arena as we were all there for a mutual purpose at the same time. We found ourselves in conversations with people in front of us, behind us, and on either side. We were all singing the words to the familiar songs. We were all connected through this one experience with one purpose.

The song "Where my girls at?" by the group 702 had us all dancing with our hands waving in the air.

We all sang together. The roar of the crowd resonated with me, and in that moment, we were all a crew. The energy of everyone being present for one purpose and supporting each other for the same cause of having a great time as each reminisced on where they were when they first heard a song being performed. We all had this one thing in common; we all knew the same songs and we sang together in community as a crew. It was powerful.

EIGHT STEPS TO FINDING YOUR CREW

One of the most powerful steps you can take in your healing journey is to seek out supportive relationships and engage in authentic communication. As you may recall our earlier discussion of the polyvagal theory, that social connections activate the ventral vagal, fostering feelings of safety and belonging. Connecting with others who understand and empathize with your experiences can provide you with immense comfort and strength. It is not just about having people around you but rather is about finding those who truly get you and can provide you with the right kind of support. Here are eight steps to help get you started.

STEP 1

Start by making a list of people in your life who make you feel safe and valued. They may be friends, family members, or even members of a support group.

STEP 2

Look for those who listen without judgment, offer empathy, and have respect for your boundaries. It's important to feel heard and understood, especially when sharing difficult or painful experiences. Surrounding yourself with supportive people can help you feel less isolated and more connected.

STEP 3

Once you have made your list, engaging in authentic communication is going to be key to building and maintaining these relationships. Ensuring that you are being honest and open about your wants, needs, and expectations of them, while also reflecting on your intentions. Authentic communication helps to build trust and deepen connections, making it easier for others to support you in meaningful ways.

STEP 4

Establish clear boundaries. Take some time to reflect on what makes you feel safe, respected, and valued, ensuring that you have a clear understanding of your needs and limits. Then communicate these needs clearly and assertively. Use "I" statements to express your needs and feelings without blaming or accusing others. For example, when you raise your voice, I feel scared.

STEP 5

Consider joining support groups or communities where you can connect with others who have similar experiences. This can be in person or online. In both cases you want to do your due diligence and make sure there are well-established rules to keep the group space safe. Participating in these groups can create a sense of belonging and understanding that is often hard to find elsewhere. The more opportunities you have to share your story with people who have walked a similar path, the more you will feel validated and empowered. It reminds you that you are not alone and that there is hope for healing. It is important to note, sharing the details of the trauma event is not recommended outside of the therapeutic setting. This retelling can be triggering and create a reliving of the experience of sorts without having the tools to manage the residual feelings.

STEP 6

Be patient with yourself as you navigate through this journey. Stepping outside your comfort zone and building supportive relationships while learning to communicate authentically takes time and practice.

STEP 7

Celebrate the small victories along the way. Oftentimes we tend to overlook the small accomplishments and feel as though nothing is working. Every little step is meaningful and should be acknowledged along the way.

STEP 8

Be kind to yourself during setbacks. Setbacks will happen, so be patient. Healing is not a linear process, and every step you take toward connection and authenticity is a step toward a healthier, more fulfilling life. It's okay to take small steps when it comes to opening up. You don't have to share everything all at once. Start with what feels manageable and gradually share more as you feel comfortable. The goal is to create a space where you can be yourself without fear of judgment or rejection. This process might take time, but it's an important part of healing and rebuilding trust in your relationships and creating your crew.

PATIENCE IS KEY

Meeting new people can be nerve-wracking for any-one, but if you've experienced trauma, that uneasiness can feel tenfold. It's completely normal to feel a bit anxious or uncomfortable in social situations, espe-cially when past experiences have made you more cautious or wary.

Your body and mind may still be on high alert, and navigating these new interactions might trigger feelings of vulnerability. The pressure to make a good impression or to fit in can feel overwhelming when you're already dealing with the echoes of past trauma.

It's important to recognize that these feelings are valid and to be kind to yourself as you face them. Taking small, manageable steps can help make the process less daunting. You can start with low-pressure settings where you can gradually get used to engaging with new people at your own pace. Keep at the forefront of your mind that everyone has their own struggles and insecurities, and you're not alone in feeling this way. By acknowledging your discomfort and taking gradual steps, you're giving yourself the space to heal and con-nect with others in a way that feels safe and genuine.

It can also be helpful to remember that each in-teraction is a chance to learn and grow not a test you need to pass. Building connections with new people is not about perfection; it's okay to stumble or feel awkward at times. Sometimes, the most meaningful relationships start with small, imperfect conversations.

Be patient and gentle with yourself and allow space for these experiences to take place naturally. Over time, these small steps can lead to a greater sense of comfort and confidence in social situations, and maybe even to taking bigger leaps to connect and rebuild trust in yourself and others.

EXERCISE: CONNECTION CHALLENGE

This exercise will help you to build confidence and practice initiating conversations with new people.

1. **Find a Quiet Space**: Choose a peaceful, comfortable place where you can focus.
2. **Set a Goal**: Decide to meet and connect with at least three new people in the next week.
3. **Prepare Your Introduction**: Think of a brief, engaging way to introduce yourself. Include your name and a fun fact or hobby. Example: "Hi, I'm [Your Name]. I love hiking and recent-

ly completed a trail that was both challenging and rewarding!"

4. **Choose Your Venues**: Pick one or more of the following places to visit where meeting new people is likely:

   o Community Events: Attend local festivals, fairs, or charity events. They often have a relaxed atmosphere and are great for striking up conversations.

   o Classes or Workshops: Sign up for a cooking class, art workshop, or fitness session. Shared interests can be a natural conversation starter.

   o Volunteering: Join a local volunteer group. Working together for a cause can build quick connections.

   o Meetup Groups: Explore Meetup.com for groups that align with your interests. It's a great way to find people who share your passions.

   o Networking Events: Go to professional or casual networking events in your area. These are specifically designed for meeting new people.

   o Cafés or Bookstores: Spend some time in a local café or bookstore where people often linger and chat. Look for book clubs or discussion groups.

5. **Practice Conversation Starters**: Before going out, practice a few conversation starters. Examples:
   o "What brings you here today?"
   o "Have you been to this event before?"
   o "I noticed you're reading [Book Title]. What do you think of it?"

6. **Reflect**: After each interaction, take a moment to jot down what went well and what you might improve. Celebrate your successes and learn from each experience.

Tip: Remember to be yourself and stay open.

CHAPTER 10: CONNECT WITH YOUR DESTINY

"You are the designer of your destiny; you are the author of your story."

—Lisa Nichols

"It's time for you to move, realizing that the thing you are seeking is also seeking you."

—Iyanla Vanzant

This journey has been about understanding yourself and your experiences on a deeper level. It's about giving language to your emotions, the struggles within your body, and the roadblocks to reaching your desires.

When we are navigating through brain fog, experiencing unexplained pain and body aches, reacting blindly to baggage and expectations that aren't ours to carry, and letting shattered stories dictate our future, healing and growth can seem like impossible pipe dreams. But when we gain clarity and understanding about what is actually going on with our brains, bodies, stories, and emotions, we realize that healing and growth are very much within our reach.

NAME IT TO UNDERSTAND IT

Expanding your vocabulary opens doors to new perspectives, new ways of thinking and the courage to embrace change. As you encounter unfamiliar experiences, words, and concepts, you start to move outside of your comfort zone, which opens the pathway for growth and development. The emergence of curiosity, compassion, and exploration enriches your understanding of yourself and the world around you.

The expansion of your vocabulary isn't just about adding new words; it's also about challenging the limitations of language itself which puts limitations upon yourself. Sometimes, the most profound experiences defy words altogether, leaving you grappling with how to articulate what happened. Now the door is open for exploring the edges that create such discomfort, and push against its boundaries to gain a deeper meaning of yourself and the world around you.

So, embrace this journey of connecting to your true destiny. Dive into books, conversations, and experiences that challenge and inspire you. Allow yourself to be curious, vulnerable, and open to the infinite possibilities that a new way of living can offer. And remember, your past is static; it can't be changed. We lose time by living in the past and in the future, leaving us to stay in a loop and miss the experiences of the now. To be in the present is giving yourself a fair shot to evolve and reflect on your journey through life in this dynamic way.

COMMIT TO YOURSELF

It is essential to make a commitment to yourself. If you don't do it, who will? It is important for you to know that reaching this point in your journey is a significant milestone. You've laid the foundation to change your life for the better. Now it's time to commit to building on that foundation.

It's time to recognize that your brain and body have always been protecting you and keeping you safe. Perhaps your brain did its best to mentally distance you from a traumatic event or events. Maybe shock caused your body to freeze or shut down as a protective measure. Even if these measures created challenges of their own, it's important to express gratitude to your brain and body for their efforts to safeguard you.

You are now in a position to reshape your daily experiences. This work is challenging and often painful, but it is also life changing. You have the capacity to thrive not just survive. Embrace the process, acknowledge the difficulty, and remember that you can do the hard thing necessary to overcome these obstacles.

Being kind to yourself and changing the tone of your inner dialogue can significantly impact your healing journey. Self-compassion is a key factor for resilience and will enhance your emotional well-being and promote a healthier relationship with yourself. When you speak to yourself with kindness and understanding, you reinforce your commitment to personal growth and self-improvement.

I can't say it enough: The difficulty of doing this work can quickly get in the way of you choosing you. There will be moments of struggle, pain, and tears. However, each step you take is a testament to your strength and determination. Don't give up on yourself; you deserve to experience a life that is different from what you have known. Commit to yourself, stand up for yourself, and keep moving forward.

THE DEEP WORK

Let's talk about doing the deep work. For those of you that have experienced the therapeutic process before, while you may have felt better at the time of completion, you may have later discovered that there is still something emotionally tugging on you, and you just can't quite figure out where this is coming from. You are seeking the long-lasting, lifetime type change, and there are transformational therapies that will help you to achieve this. What is key is your willingness to learn how to navigate the intense emotions as you are experiencing the therapy process.

The kind of deep work I'm speaking of involves delving far into the root causes of any psychological issues, unresolved trauma, and emotional wounds, which often stem from trauma from your childhood or past relationships. An essential component to doing intensive work is identifying and challenging your deeply held beliefs about yourself and the world around you. These beliefs, oftentimes negative or limiting in nature, may have been formed as maladaptive coping mechanisms which you may have found hindering your personal growth and mental health.

By concentrating on understanding how these experiences impact your current behavior, emotional responses and your self-perception, will also begin to help you connect to the wounded part of you. The therapy world, while it has its challenges, has grown leaps and bounds with amazing techniques to dive into the subconscious mind, where those unresolved conflicts and fears take hold like a squatter in an abandoned building.

A few of these techniques for you to seek out, as mentioned before, are EMDR (Eye Movement Desensitization and Reprocessing), Internal Family Systems (IFS), and mindfulness practices so you can dive deep into the crevices of the subconscious.

Brainspotting, polyvagal exercises, sensorimotor approach to psychotherapy, and somatic therapy are additional possibilities for you to explore the core issues. At the time of this writing, the newest approach, ketamine-assisted therapy, allows collaboration with a medical professional and psychotherapist. Ketamine, a dissociative anesthetic, is to treat conditions like depression, PTSD, and anxiety, with the medical professional administering the drug and the psychotherapist guiding the therapeutic process.

Being aware of these types of therapies will help you find the right therapist.

Ultimately, what we want is enlightenment! The more you can recognize patterns of behavior and the thoughts that may go unnoticed, the better chances you will have to change the way you respond to situations and relationships.

Unlike supportive therapy, the deep work involves being with uncomfortable emotions—grief, anger, shame, guilt, or fear—rather than pushing them away. We want you to grow and find relief rather than avoid the feelings. The intensive therapeutic process will help you understand the source and the role of these emotions in your life.

HEALING EQUALS FREEDOM

Releasing what no longer serves you, or what simply does not belong to you, is a profound act of honoring yourself. By letting go of these burdens, you signal to yourself that freedom is possible. There is a deep sense of freedom that overcomes you in the healing process. In a time when women face unprecedented challenges to their freedoms, embarking on a journey toward healing becomes an unassailable act of self-empowerment. Your healing is yours alone, and much like your education and values, no one can ever take it from you.

The freedom that comes from healing is best described as transformative. It allows you to shed the weight of past traumas, negative beliefs, and harmful patterns. As you release these, you make space for new, positive experiences and a healthier, more fulfilling life. Healing frees you from the chains of the past, enabling you to live more fully in the present and to face the future with hope and confidence.

As you heal, confidence naturally begins to emerge. This newfound self-assurance stems from the understanding that you are no longer defined by your past wounds or the limitations others have placed on you. You start to see yourself in a new light, recognizing your strengths and capabilities. This confidence empowers you to set boundaries, pursue your goals, and live authentically.

Healing also brings a sense of inner peace and stability. When you let go of what no longer serves you, you create balance within yourself. This inner calm radiates outward, influencing your relationships and interactions with others. You become more steadfast, better able to handle life's challenges, and more compassionate towards yourself as you experience them.

The journey of healing is a testament to your strength and perseverance. Every step you take into the unknown is a step towards victory. By committing to your healing, you reclaim your power and take control of your life and no longer become a prisoner of your past. A liberated you is an empowered you, so get ready to embrace the fullness of your potential.

STEPPING INTO THE LIBERATED YOU

Now let's just take a deep breath, my friend. You're not alone in this journey. Your superpower lies in your ability to assemble a crew that supports you unconditionally and is truly *for* you. If no one has told you yet, and you haven't said it to yourself, let me remind you: YOU ARE AMAZING. The bravery you've shown in choosing to confront the scariest parts of your past is nothing short of heroic, warrior-like even. Those old burdens and emotional baggage now have your permission to be left behind.

As you step into your liberated self, remember that you possess the capability to discover and fulfill your life's purpose. The clarity you gain through the healing process opens up a world of possibilities. Embrace this newfound clarity and let it guide you toward your true path. Your journey has equipped you with the tools and resilience needed to face any future challenges with confidence and grace. Trust the process, and in turn you will begin to trust yourself. Remember you have made it this far, and you are still here!

As you continue, allow yourself to dream big and pursue your passions with vigor. The liberation you will feel is the key to unlocking your wildest imagination. Every time you show up for yourself, it speaks to what you are capable of; your strength and determination is unprecedented. Your past does not define you; it will be the choices you make now and for the future that will define and create who you are to be in this life.

This is the beginning of an exciting new chapter in your life. Step boldly into your future taking this newfound clarity and purpose and run like you are on the last leg of an Olympic race. Celebrate your journey, cherish your growth, and embrace the liberated, empowered you.

The world is waiting for your unique gifts and contributions. Go forth with confidence, knowing that you are capable, worthy, and deserving of all the wonderful things life has to offer.

EXERCISE: THE DESTINY DISCOVERY MAP

This exercise helps you clarify your aspirations, stay motivated, and align your actions with your broader vision for a fulfilling and purposeful life.

1. **Find a Quiet Space**: Choose a peaceful, comfortable place where you can focus.

2. **Gather Materials**

   o Large piece of paper or a poster board

   o Colored markers, pens, or pencils

   o Sticky notes or index cards

   o A ruler (optional)

   o Tape or glue

3. **Draw the Map**

   o On your large piece of paper or poster board, draw a large circle in the center. This will be your Destiny Hub.

   o Around this central circle, draw several smaller circles or clusters. These will represent key areas of your life or aspects related to your destiny (e.g., career, relationships, personal growth, health, hobbies).

4. **Reflect on Key Areas of Your Life**

   o Think about the main areas that are important for your destiny. These might include your career aspirations, personal relationships, health goals, or personal passions.

- o Write down these key areas on separate sticky notes or index cards.
- o Place the sticky notes or index cards in the appropriate circles around the Destiny Hub. Arrange them according to their importance or relevance to your overall vision.

5. **Define Your Vision**
   - o Visualize Each Area
     - ▪ In each smaller circle, write or draw what your ideal outcome looks like for that area. Be specific and detailed.
     - ▪ For each key area, describe what achieving your ideal outcome would look and feel like. What are the specific goals or milestones?
   - o Connect the Dots
     - ▪ Draw lines connecting the smaller circles to the Destiny Hub. These lines represent how each area contributes to your overall destiny.
     - ▪ Reflect on how each area influences or supports the others. How do they interrelate in achieving your broader vision?

6. **Identify Key Actions**

   o Set goals for each area. Identify specific, actionable goals that will help you move towards your ideal outcome.

   o Write down these goals on separate sticky notes or index cards and place them near the corresponding circles on your map.

   o Write down the steps you need to take to achieve each goal. Include timelines and resources needed.

   o For each goal, outline a detailed action plan. What are the immediate next steps you can take?

7. **Visualize Your Progress**

   o Draw or place small markers on your map to represent milestones or achievements related to your goals.

   o Reflect on what milestones would indicate progress towards your destiny. How will you celebrate these achievements?

   o Schedule regular times (e.g., weekly or monthly) to review and update your Destiny Map. Adjust goals and action plans as needed.

- What progress have you made? Are there any changes or new goals that need to be added to your map?

8. **Reflect and Celebrate**

- After a set period (e.g., six months or a year), reflect on your overall progress and how your Destiny Map has guided you.
- How has working with your Destiny Map impacted your life? What have you learned about yourself and your destiny?
- Celebrate the milestones and achievements you have reached. Acknowledge your efforts and successes along the way.
- What are you most proud of? How will you continue to build on your successes and stay connected to your destiny?

This final exercise is your call to action, bringing you a step closer to living in your purpose and strengthening your confidence. This tool was created to turn abstract concepts into something more tangible and assist you on this intentional journey of breaking free of the baggage. The exercise is more than just a visual representation, it is an invitation for you to take an active role in designing the life that you are meant to live. When you map out the key areas of your life, you will gain clarity about where you are and where you want to go.

This tool not only helps you to discover more about yourself, but it enables you to be an active participant in shaping your destiny. Your creation of your roadmap will help you to define your vision, set meaningful and actionable goals.

Recognizing your progress and acknowledging your achievements throughout the journey is essential to your development. Your map should evolve as you evolve and reflect your growth. The Destiny Discovery Map will remind you to honor and remain connected to your vision and to embrace the challenges you may face along the way.

This process of healing is deeply personal and no one size will fit all. Aligning with your destiny is the driving force to shed the generational burdens and emotional baggage you have been carrying. It is your connection to your destiny that will empower you to step into your authentic self and live your life courageously.

Resources

Therapist Directories	Links
Asian Mental Health Collective	https://asianmhc.org
American Psychological Association	https://locator.apa.org
Black Female Therapists	https://www.blackfemaletherapists.com/
Choosing Therapy	https://directory.choosingtherapy.com/
Clinicians of color	https://www.cliniciansofcolor.org/find-a-therapist/
EMDR Therapist	https://www.emdria.org/find-an-emdr-therapist/
Good Therapy	https://goodtherapy.org
Inclusive Therapists	https://www.inclusivetherapists.com/

International therapist directory	https:// internationaltherapistdirectory.com/
Latinx Therapy	https://latinxtherapy.com
Neurodivergent Therapists	https://ndtherapists.com/
Therapy Den	https://www.therapyden.com/
Therapy for black girls	https://therapyforblackgirls.com/
Therapist.com	https://therapist.com/
Therapy Tribe	https://www.therapytribe.com/
Psychology Today	https://www.psychologytoday.com/us
Open Path Collective	https://openpathcollective.org
Zencare	https://zencare.co/

Bibliography

American Psychological Association. (n.d.). *Trauma*. https://www.apa.org/topics/trauma/

Calhoun, L. G., & Tedeschi, R. G. (2006). *The foundations of posttraumatic growth: New considerations.* Psychological Inquiry, 15(1), 1-18, https://doi.org/10.1207/s15327965pli1501_01.

Creswell, Akil. Interview by Dr. Laryssa Creswell. May 2024.

Dana, D. (2020). *Polyvagal exercises for safety and connection: 50 client-centered practices.* W. W. Norton & Company.

Schwartz, R. C. (2021). *No bad parts: Healing trauma and restoring wholeness with the internal family systems model.* Sounds True.

Schwartz, R. C., & Sweezy, M. (2019). *Internal family systems therapy* (2nd ed.). Guilford Press.

van der Kolk, Bessel (2014). *The Body Keeps the Score: Brain, Mind, and Body in the Healing of Trauma.* Penguin Books.

About the Author

Laryssa M. Creswell, Ed.D., MT-BC, LCPC, LPMT, ACS, brings over two decades of expertise in mental health treatment to her private practice, where she specializes in trauma-focused therapy for women and teen girls. As a board-certified music therapist and licensed clinical professional counselor in Maryland and DC, Dr. Creswell has dedicated her career to empowering individuals through therapeutic interventions.

With extensive experience across diverse mental health settings, Dr. Creswell's journey began as a music therapist, serving individuals across the lifespan. Her commitment to improving treatment methodologies led her to focus on developing tailored programs for women and teen girls grappling with anxiety, depression, and trauma.

Beyond her clinical work, Dr. Creswell is a passionate advocate for advancing mental health research. She has authored studies exploring women's perspectives on psychiatric treatment and is poised to delve deeper into this vital area of inquiry. Dr. Creswell's holistic approach and dedication to innovation make her a trusted guide on the path to healing and resilience.